Basic
Sailing
Skills

by Sven Donaldson

Published by: Canadian Yachting Association
1600 James Naismith Drive
Gloucester, Ont.
K1B 5N4
Tel   613-748-5687
Fax 613-748-5688
ISBN 0-920232-17-5

Cover Photograph: Brian Jeun-Conway
                   Sail Nepean Sailing School

Layout and Design: Cameron Kennedy & Associates Limited

Canadian Yachting Association is a member of the
International Sailing Schools Association (ISSA).

WARNING

This handbook is only part of the Canadian Yachting Association's White Sail Levels I - III program. On its own, it cannot provide adequate training for safe sailing. Please contact the Canadian Yachting Association for further information on sail training in your area. Phone 613-748-5687.

Acknowledgements

David Langdon, *Chairman Learn to Sail Committee,* and **Peter Wood,** *Technical Director Training Division* played central roles in the creation of this new White Sail manual. Certainly, without their diligent efforts, the project would never have left the dock.

The following other people—all members of the CYA Learn to Sail Committee—reviewed drafts of the text and offered valuable suggestions: David Baird, Marc Chagnon, Byron Salahor, Todd Hataley, Will MacKeen, Alexa Bagnell and Agnes McLean. My sincere thanks to all these dedicated volunteers.

S. D.

CYA Provincial Sailing Associations

British Columbia Sailing
Alberta Sailing Association
Saskatchewan Sailing Clubs Association
Manitoba Sailing Association
Ontario Sailing Association
Fédération de voile du Quebec
New Brunswick Sailing Association
Nova Scotia Yachting Association
Prince Edward Island Sailing Association
Newfoundland and Labrador Sailing Association

Basic

Sailing

Skills

Official Manual of the CYA White Sail Standard

Introductory Book of the CYA "Sailing Skills" series

Contains:
Getting to Know your Boat
Setting up for Sailing
First Skills
Basic Sail Adjustments
Sailing Terminology
Sailing Safety
Over 60 illustrations and Drawings

Also available:
Advanced Sailing Skills
Official manual of the CYA Bronze Sail Standard
International Handbook Learn to Sail

CYA has national training standards in:
Learn to Cruise
Learn to Windsurf
Learn to Power Boat
Race Officer
Race Judge

Each of these programs has an official training manual to
support the training program.

Canadian Yachting Association publications are available from:

Canadian Yachting Association
Provincial Sailing Associations
Book and Marine Supply Stores

Preface

Basic Sailing Skills is the first in a series of manuals which are used as the student text book in the Canadian Yachting Association's Learn to Sail Program. The original *Basic Sailing Skills* was written in 1974 by Don Giffin, an active instructor, Albacore racing competitor and dedicated volunteer. Over the next seventeen years it was used extensively by over 30,000 sailors as they were introduced to the jargon and theory of sailing.

In 1990 the Learn to Sail Committee of the Canadian Yachting Association decided to have *Basic Sailing Skills* rewritten to reflect the changes which had taken place in sailing over the past seventeen years.

Sven Donaldson, a Vancouver based sailing writer, was commissioned by the Canadian Yachting Association to write this new version of *Basic Sailing Skills*. Sven has two other sailing books to his credit (*A Sailors Guide to Sails* and the *New Sail Theory*) as well as many articles in *Pacific Yachting Magazine, Sail, and Cruising World*. In *Basic Sailing Skills*, Sven has simplified terminology so the reader gets a hands on appreciation of the enjoyment of sailing.

Cedric Burgers, a CYA senior sailing instructor and University of British Columbia architecture student from Vancouver drew the illustrations. The illustrations provide a level of detail rarely shown in other sailing instructional books. The sequence of drawings for the step progression of skills should make it easier for anyone learning to tack or gybe.

Finally I would like to thank the members of the Learn to Sail Committee who were supportive in their review of the various versions of the draft. The members are: David Langdon, *Chairman*, David Baird, Nicholas Breyfogle, Marc Chagnon, Todd Hataley, Will MacKeen. I would also like to thank Agnes McLean, *Vice-President Training*, and Brian Lane, *Executive Director*, for their encouragement of this project.

Peter Wood,
Technical Director Training Division.

TABLE OF CONTENTS

Acknowledgements 3

Preface 5

Chapter 1   **Using this Book** 10

Chapter 2   **Your First Sail: What It Might Be Like** . . .12

Chapter 3   **About Learning the Sailing Language** . .15

Chapter 4   **Getting to Know Your Boat** 16

           Orientation and Directions 20

           Types of Sailboats 21

Chapter 5   **Steering Clear of Trouble** 23

           The Boat as Safe Refuge 23

           Dressing for Safety and Comfort 24

           Hypothermia 25

           Electric Shock Hazards 25

           Sunburn, Eye Damage,

               and Overheating 27

           The Self-Reliant Sailor 27

Chapter 6   **Sensing the Wind** 28

           Feeling Wind 30

           Talking About Wind Direction 30

           Gusts and Lulls .31

Chapter 7   **Setting Up for Sailing** 32

           Collecting the Parts 32

           Preparing the Hull 32

           Facing the Boat Upwind 35

           Rigging the Sails .36

           Checking the Safety Gear 39

           Knots and Related Skills 39

Chapter 8   **Out on the Water: First Skills** 42

           Skipper-Crew Teamwork 42

           Getting Underway 44

           Launching off a Beach or Ramp 45

           Underway from a Dock 45

           Steering With the Tiller 46

How to Steer Using Clues
   from the Sails 47
Steering with the Help of Ticklers 48
In to Go and Out to Slow 49
When the Wind Tips the Boat 51

Chapter 9   **Basic Sail Adjustments** 52
Playing the Sail .52
If in Doubt, Sheet Out 53
Sail Trimming with Ticklers 54
Sailing Higher and Lower Courses 55
Learning to Steer a Straight Course 56
Trimming Main and Jib Together 57

Chapter 10   **Learning to Come About** 58
Busting Through the "No Go Zone" 59
Skipper's Actions for Coming About 60
Hand Exchange Without a
   Tiller Extension 63
Crew's Actions Coming About 63
Getting Out of Irons 64

Chapter 11   **Learning to Gybe** 65
The Gybe Path 66
Gybing Details: Roles for Skipper
   and Crew 67
Accidental Gybes and "Laser" Gybes 67

Chapter 12   **Back to Shore** .68
Dock Landings 68
Beach Landings .70
Putting the Boat to Bed 71
Sail Care 71

Chapter 13   **Going Places by Sailboat** 72
Port Tack, Starboard Tack 74
Sailors' Word Games 75

Chapter 14   **Upwind Sailing Skills** 77
How Close to Haul? 78
When and How to Come About 78
Controlling Heel .79

Chapter 15 Reaching and Downwind Skills 81

Adjusting the Centreboard or
  Daggerboard 81
Using The Boom Vang 82
Coordinating Trim and Tiller 83
Sailing Wing-on-Wing 84
Sailing by the Lee 85
Gybing in Stronger Winds 86

Chapter 16 Launching and Landing Challenges 87

Getting off the Beach in an
  Onshore Wind 87
Downwind Beach Landings 88
To and From the Windward Side
  of a Dock 89
Sailing from a Mooring 90

Chapter 17 Capsize and Man Overboard 90

Righting a Capsized Boat 90
Turning Turtle and What to Do About It . . . 93
Man Overboard 94
Treating Hypothermia 95

Chapter 18 The Importance of Seamanship 96

Sharing the Water with Other Boats 96
Evaluating Weather Conditions 98
Wind and Waves 100
Geographic Hazards 100
When the Wind Quits 101

Chapter 19 Going On in Sailing 103

Additional CYA Sail Training 103
Other Sailing Opportunities 104

Appendix: White Sail Level I, II & III Standards 105

Sailing Glossary 113

Chapter 1 — Using this Book

So you want to learn to sail? Great, let's get started! This book is like a travel guide—your passport to the world of sailing. Chances are you'll be reading it as part of a learn-to-sail program run by CYA certified instructors. This is definitely the way to go, because, like most active sports, there's a lot to sailing that must be learned by "doing" and can't be picked up from the pages of a book.

But even with the help of a good instructor, some aspects of sailing may seem confusing to the newcomer. Here's where this book comes in handy. Use it to review what you learn from your instructor and to read ahead so you'll know what to expect next. At the end of most chapters are review questions that will help you learn what you'll need to know to meet the CYA White Sail Standards Levels I, II and III. In the appendix at the end of the book are the White Sail Standards themselves, a glossary of sailing words, and a list of other books you can read for more information about sailing. There's also an index to help you locate information on particular topics more quickly.

Chapter 2 — Your First Sail: What It Might Be Like

The best way to become a sailor is to go sailing, so the White Sail program is designed to get you out on the water as quickly and as often as possible. Unless you have bad luck with the weather, your first sail will probably take place on your first day of class and might go something like this:

It's been a nice, sunny day and the afternoon breeze is just starting to lighten off for the evening. Down on the beach, the students in your sailing class are grouped around a sailboat, watching and asking questions while an instructor shows you how to set up the boat and prepare it for launching.

The training boats for your class each have two sails held up by a vertical, aluminium pole called the **mast**. "This little sail ahead of the mast is called the **jib**" the instructor explains, "... and this bigger one behind the mast is the **mainsail**."

Next, she points to a couple of ropes attached to the lower, rear corner of the jib. "These lines are called the **jib sheets**" she says. "When the wind is blowing across the boat from one side," she explains, "you pull on the opposite jib sheet." She goes on to show you the **mainsheet** — a line and pulley arrangement attached to the boom which controls the mainsail. She also points out the **tiller**, a wooden handle at the back of the boat used for steering.

"You've already learned enough to try sailing", says your instructor with a smile. "Who wants to go first?" Nobody steps forward, so she glances over the group and chooses (Gulp) you!

Before you've really had time to think, the boat has been wheeled into the water and floated off its launching cart. Standing in water a little above your knees, you hold onto the edge of its **hull** while your instructor makes a couple of adjustments to the equipment. Then she holds the boat while you scramble in and crouch down low in the **cockpit**. All the while, the sails — main and jib — have been streaming downwind, fluttering like flags because the sheets which control them are slack. The instructor hops aboard behind you and hands you one of the jib sheets, saying "Pull in the jib and hold it". As you do so, she **sheets** in the mainsail.

The results are dramatic. At once, the boat seems to wake up, changing in an instant from a floating clutter of cloth, rope and hardware into an almost living thing. The noisy flapping of the sails abruptly ceases, and the boat quietly scoots away, going from a standstill to a brisk pace in a matter of seconds. It's a great feeling.

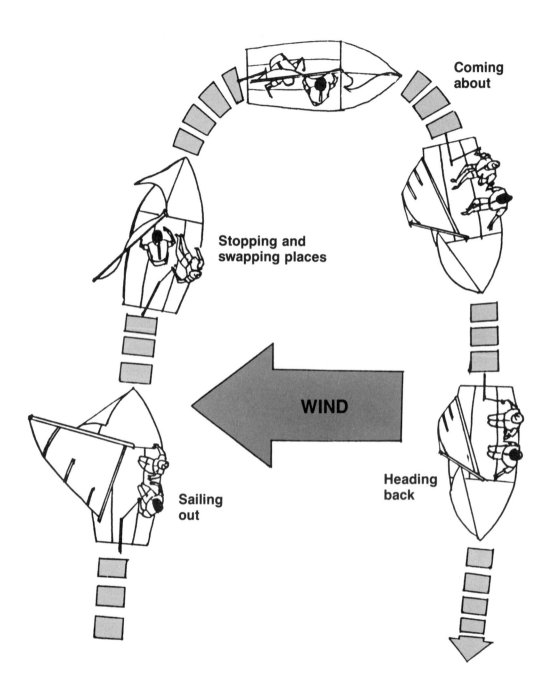

Coming about

Stopping and swapping places

Sailing out

WIND

Heading back

Diagram 1) Your First Sail

After a few moments you realize that you're still crouching low in hull while your instructor is perched on the edge of the boat with her back to the wind. ''Come up here on the **windward side**'', she says, and as you move to sit beside her, she shifts her weight inward a bit to keep the boat level. From here, you can see much better and the sensation of effortless speed is even stronger.

''Now let's stop'', she says. ''Just release the jib sheet and shift your body weight toward the middle of the boat''. You release the jib sheet while your instructor eases out the mainsheet and the sails start to flap again. Without the force of the wind in the sails, the boat begins to tip, but you quickly slide your body toward the center of the cockpit to level it out.

''Now you try steering,'' says your instructor, and as the boat sits still in water with its sails flapping, the two of you swap places. Once you're positioned properly with your back to the wind and your rear hand on the tiller, the instructor sheets in and the boat is off again — this time with you at the helm!

In the next few minutes you discover the basics of steering a sailboat. You learn to alternately push the tiller gently toward the boom until the sails are almost ready to flap, then pull the tiller back slightly, taking your clues from what the sails are doing. When it's time to head back to the beach, you make the boat **come about** by pushing the tiller toward the sail and holding it there as boat turns, sails flapping, until the wind fills them from the other side.

Before you know it, you're back on shore while your instructor takes another student out for a spin. The assistant instructor is explaining something about raising and lowering the rudder blade, but you're only half listening. Instead, you're thinking back to the way the boat felt as it slid quietly along and starting to see why so many people love sailing ...

Chapter 3 — About Learning the Sailing Language

Sailors don't talk like other folks, at least when they're around boats, so if your going to become a sailor you've got to learn some "sailor words". Sure you could try to get along by pointing and describing, but the fact is you won't get much further in sailing without a sailing vocabulary than you'd get on a hiking trip through South America without some Spanish.

But don't worry. If you've read the first chapter, you've already picked up about a dozen important sailing words and you'll quickly learn a lot more as you go along. Any time you run across a word you don't know, check the glossary at the back of this book (page 113) or ask your instructor. To get you off to a good start, the next chapter offers a quick tour of a sailboat and its basic equipment.

Chapter 4 — Getting to Know Your Boat

Key Ideas:
- Sailing Dinghies
- Parts and Their Jobs
- Onboard Orientation
- Other Types of Sailboats

Learn-to-sail programs often use **sloop rigged dinghies** such as Flying Juniors, 420s, Echos, CLs, Albacores, Mirrors, and Pirates. "Sloop rigged" means that a boat has one mast and two sails: the main and the jib. "Dinghy" just means a small boat that carries, at most, three people. A typical training dinghy and it's equipment are diagrammed and described on the following two pages.

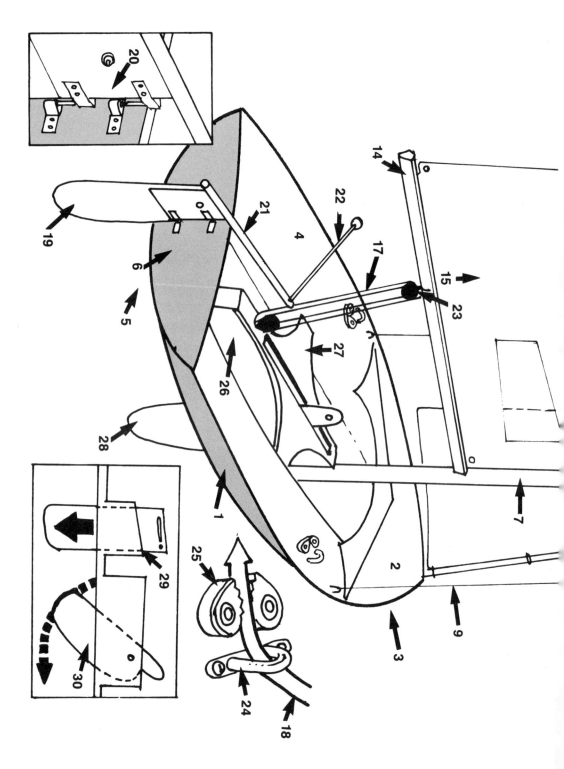

Diagram 2) Parts of a Sailboat

1) *Hull* - Shell or body of the boat.
2) *Deck* - Flat upper "lid" covering parts of the hull.
3) *Bow* - Front of boat.
4) *Cockpit* - Recess in the hull where sailors sit.
5) *Stern* - Back of boat.
6) *Transom* - Part of hull extending across the stern.
7) *Mast* - Vertical spar that holds sails up.
8) *Forestay* - Mast support wire leading to bow.
9) *Shrouds* - Mast support wires leading to hull sides.
10) *Turnbuckle* - Shroud tension adjustor.
11) *Clevis pin* - Removable link between turnbuckle / hull.
12) *Cotter pin* - Locks clevis pin in place.
13) *Shackle* - U-shaped metal link closed with a clevis pin.
14) *Boom* - Horizontal spar at bottom of mainsail.
15) *Mainsail* - Large sail set behind the mast
16) *Jib* - Small sail set ahead of mast
17) *Mainsheet* - Controls angle between mainsail / boat.
18) *Jib sheet* - Controls angle between jib / boat.
19) *Rudder* - Steering blade mounted on transom.
20) *Gudgeons / Pintles* - Mating parts of rudder hinges.
21) *Tiller* - Handle attached to top of rudder.
22) *Tiller Extension* - Secondary handle on the tiller.
23) *Blocks* - Sea going pulleys.
24) *Fairleads* - Keep lines from getting tangled.
25) *Cleats* - Grip and hold lines
26) *Centreboard trunk* - Houses centreboard (CB).
27) *Thwart* - Supports top of CB trunk and provides a seat.
28) *Centreboard-Daggerboard* - Blade that projects into water to stop side slipping.
29) *Daggerboard lifts vertically.*
30) *Centreboard swings back and up.*

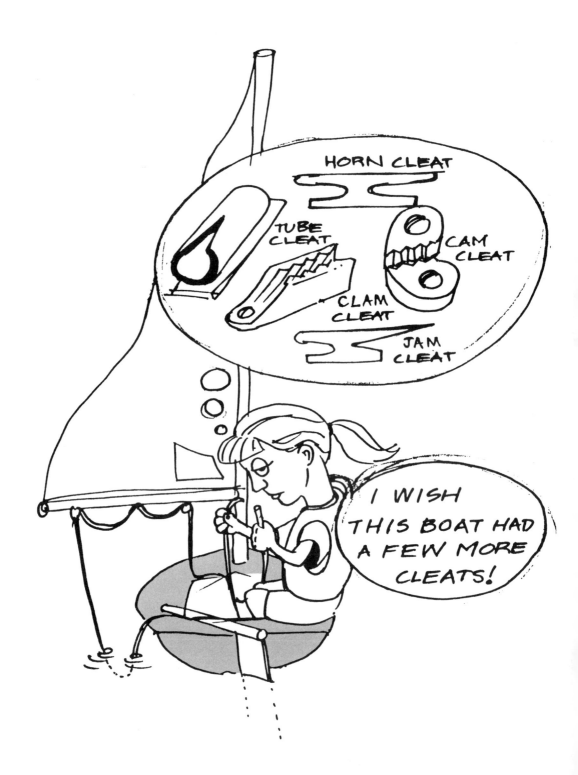

Orientation and Directions

When you're on a boat, there are some special words that help you find your way around. If you stand on a boat facing the bow, **port** means left and **starboard** means right. It's a sailor's custom to associate port with the colour red and starboard with the colour green for navigation lights, buoys and so forth. The fact that "port", "left" and "red" are short words, while "starboard", "right" and "green" are all longer is a handy memory aid.

Diagram 3) Directions on a boat

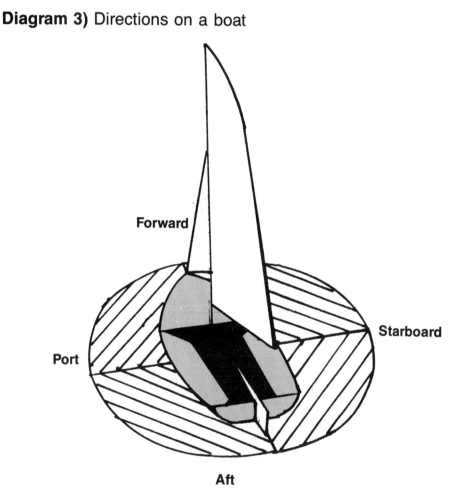

Forward

Starboard

Port

Aft

Forward means toward the bow, regardless of how you, the sailor are facing. **Aft** means toward the stern. By using these words, you'll avoid confusion whenever two sailors happen to be facing in different directions.

Types of Sailboats

Not all sail training boats are sloops. Some are **cat rigged** which means they have only a mainsail rather than both main and jib. Among the most popular cat rigged boats are Lasers, Optimists, Sabots, and Sunfish.

Sailboards are something like sailboats and something like surfboards. This dynamic sport needs some special skills that you won't get from a basic sailing program. If you want to learn how, it's best to enroll in a training program taught by a CYA certified windsurfing instructor.

Sail training programs for adults are often taught on **keelboats**. These are usually larger than dinghies and are equipped with a heavy underwater fin called a **keel** in place of a centreboard.

Finally, there are **catamarans** or double hulled sailboats. Often called **cats** for short, they are, in fact, usually rigged as sloops. Like sailboards, catamarans are exceptionally fast and exciting. The best known type is the Hobie 16, but there are many others.

Diagram 4) Types of sailboats

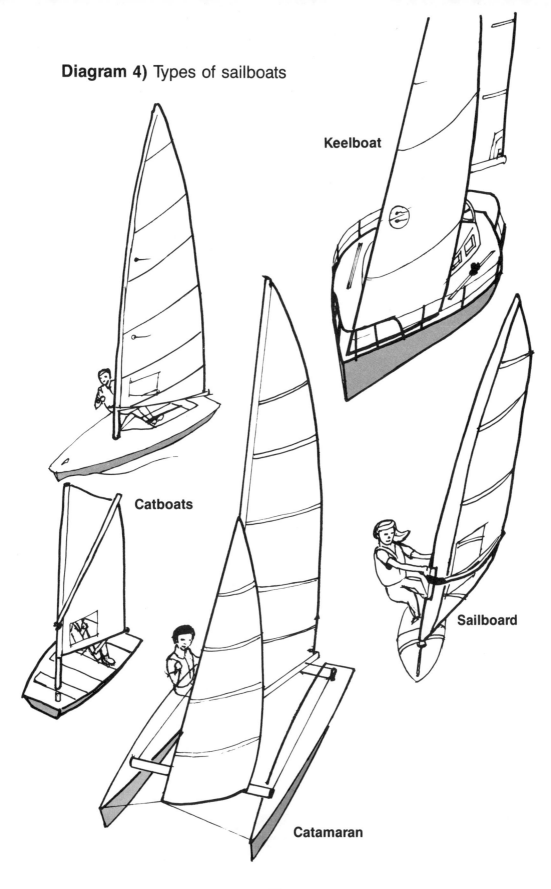

Keelboat

Catboats

Sailboard

Catamaran

CHAPTER 5 — Steering Clear of Trouble

Key Ideas:
- Stay With the Boat
- Personal Floatation
- Keeping Warm
- Electrical Hazards
- Sun and Heat Problems

Sailing is a very safe sport as long as you use good judgement and obey a few basic safety rules. When you first start out, you should sail under the supervision of a qualified instructor who can ensure that the sailing area is safe and the conditions suitable.

In sailing, there are five principle hazards you should know about: drowning, cold (hypothermia), electric shock, overheating and sunburn. Here's how to protect yourself from them:

The Boat as Safe Refuge

It's important to remember that even a small sailboat can very quickly take you far from land — much too far to swim back if you get into difficulties.

Think of your boat as a kind of space capsule that's designed and equipped to protect you from the dangers of cold and deep water. Even if **swamped** (filled with water) or **capsized** (tipped on it's side), any properly equipped small sailboat has enough sealed in floatation to keep it from sinking. This floatation is usually provided by waterproof air tanks within the hull or by inflatable air bags beneath the seats.

> **Safety Rule #1 -** Always stay with your boat even if it breaks down or capsizes. (In Chapter 17 you'll learn how to upright a capsized boat and continue sailing).

Dressing for Safety and Comfort

Your second line of defense while sailing is your **PFD** or **Personal Floatation Device** which should be worn at all times. Many types have been tested by the Canadian Department of Transport (DOT), so you should be sure that the one you're using bears a DOT approved label for a person of your weight. Also be sure your PFD isn't ripped or otherwise damaged.

For rugged conditions when large waves are present, DOT approved **Life Jackets** are safer than PFDs because their high, buoyant collars keep a person floating face up, even if unconscious. However, for most inshore sailing, an approved PFD is entirely adequate and quite a bit more comfortable.

Diagram 5) Personal sailing gear

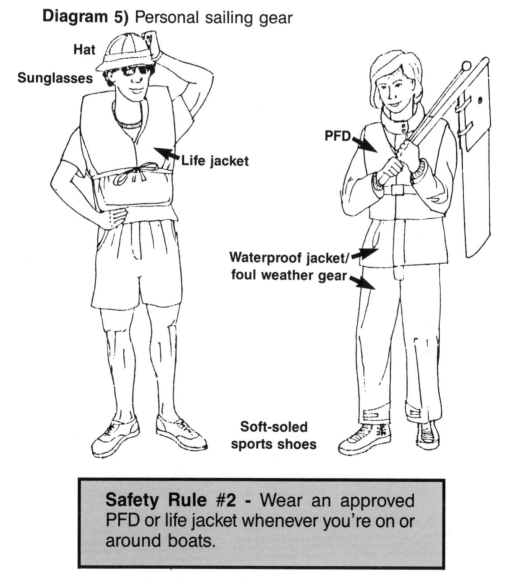

Hat

Sunglasses

Life jacket

PFD

Waterproof jacket/
foul weather gear

Soft-soled
sports shoes

Safety Rule #2 - Wear an approved PFD or life jacket whenever you're on or around boats.

Hypothermia

Even on a warm summer day it is likely to be surprisingly cool out on the water, particularly if there's a good breeze blowing. Dress warmly (or carry extra clothing) especially when the air temperature is below 21°C or the water temperature below 18°C. Generally, it's best to "overdress" because you can always take something off if you get too warm. A **waterproof jacket or foul weather gear** are very helpful because its surprisingly easy to get chilled when your clothes become wet.

Advanced sailors often wear foam rubber **wet suits** similar to the ones that divers use, or special **dry suits** which are made of waterproof material and have flexible seals at the neck, sleeves and ankles. However, as long as you're only sailing in good weather and under supervision it isn't necessary to buy this costly gear.

> **Safety Rule #3 -** Dress warmly for sailing and wear appropriate waterproof garments when conditions warrant them.

Electric Shock Hazards

Believe it or not, many of the most serious small boat sailing accidents took place before the boat even reached the water! How? By allowing the mast to touch an overhead power cable. If this happens, a powerful jolt of electricity may travel down the mast and through the bodies of sailors who are touching the boat.

Out on the water, the same thing can happen if lightning strikes the boat or if you sail into a power cable that hangs low over the water. Be on the lookout for overhead cables and return to shore at once if there are thunderstorms in the vicinity.

> **Safety Rule #4 -** Before setting up a boat in a parking lot or wheeling it down to the water, *always* check that there isn't an overhead electric cable in the way. Look out for low hanging power cables while sailing, and come in immediately if thunder clouds develop.

Diagram 6) Electrical Hazards from thunderstorms and overhead cables.

Sunburn, Eye Damage, and Overheating

The combination of long hours in the sun and reflective water puts sailors at serious risk when it comes to sunburn. Young sailors often disregard the danger, but too much sunlight has now been linked to serious skin damage and skin cancer. Don't take chances — wear a **hat** with a brim and protect exposed skin with a transparent waterproof sunblock (minimum number 15), or better yet, zinc oxide cream. Long sleeved shirts and pants are also a good idea, especially during peak sun periods (10 AM to 3 PM).

Our eyes are particularly vulnerable to sun damage, so good quality **sunglasses** with UV absorbant lenses are a sailing must. To avoid losing them overboard, they should be secured with a string or elastic strap behind the head.

Illness from excessive sun and heat may occur during hot, windless days on the water. To avoid trouble, take drinks along, keep your head covered, and return to shore if you develop a headache, faintness, nausea or excessive sweating.

> **Safety Rule #5 -** Protect your skin and eyes from the damaging effects of too much sunlight. Drink plenty of liquids on hot days and watch for signs of heat exhaustion.

The Self-Reliant Sailor

At first, while you're sailing under the close supervision of an instructor, obeying the five basic safety rules and your instructor's directions will ensure a safe, enjoyable time out on the water. Later, as you become more skilled and independent, you will need to learn about the weather, coastal geography, and sharing the water with other boats. A good sailor is self-reliant and can respond appropriately to almost any sailing situation. Chapter 17 (Capsize and Man Overboard) and Chapter 18 (Seamanship) will teach you some of the skills you'll need to sail independently.

Chapter 6 — Sensing the Wind

Key Ideas:
- Wind Direction Clues
- Upwind and Downwind
- Windward and Leeward
- Gusts and Lulls

Sailors are fascinated with wind, not only because it makes sailboats go, but because it's not easily understood. Wind is simply air movement caused by heating and cooling of the earth's atmosphere. The trouble is that you can't see air, and the way it moves can get pretty complicated.

To sail a boat, you need to know the direction the invisible wind is coming from, but how? Some of the clues to look for are:

1) Flags

2) The way sails are oriented when allowed to flap freely.

3) The orientation of **wind indicators** and weather vanes.

4) Positions of boats tied to moorings or docks. (Careful, you may be mislead if there's a strong current.)

5) Waves and ripples moving downwind on water's surface.

6) Smoke from chimneys or ship funnels.

7) Motion of low clouds. (High clouds can fool you).

Diagram 7) Wind Clues - How many indications of wind direction can you find?

Feeling the Wind

The coolness and motion of the wind can also be felt on your face, hands and the back of your neck. By paying attention to these sensations, you can learn to tell the general wind direction, even with your eyes closed.

When sailors talk about the wind they often refer to the direction from which it is blowing. When you hear someone say there's a **west wind** today, this means the wind is coming from the west.

Talking About Wind Direction

Because wind is so important in sailing, directions are often described in terms of the wind. **Upwind** means directly toward the source of the wind, while **downwind** means away from it.

You may also have heard the word **windward** which is really the two words "wind" and "toward" run together. Sailors say that one thing is windward of another if it's closer to the source of the wind, but not necessarily directly upwind. A companion word, **leeward**, means just the opposite. In sailing it will often be helpful to refer to the windward and leeward sides of the hull or the sails. To tell which is which, just remember that windward is the side that the wind reaches first.

Diagram 8) Orienting to the wind

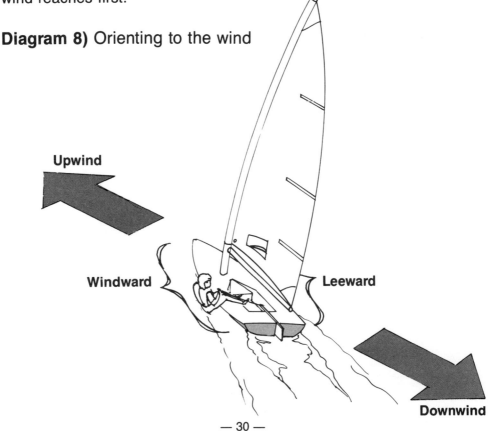

Upwind

Windward

Leeward

Downwind

Gusts and Lulls

You've probably noticed that the wind seldom blows with the same strength for very long. Instead, there are **gusts** of stronger wind that alternate with weaker **lulls**. Good sailors react to the gusts and lulls by moving their bodies and making other adjustments. This is one of the things that makes sailing a dynamic and exciting sport.

In Chapter 18 (Seamanship), you'll learn more about wind, weather and the waves. For now, practice looking for wind clues and developing your **wind sense** so that you'll know what the wind is doing whenever you're around boats and the water.

Chapter 7 — Setting Up for Sailing

Key Ideas:
- **Pepare the Hull**
- **Bow to Wind**
- **Rigging the Sails**
- **Necessary Knots**

Each day, before you go sailing, the sailboat must be set up or **rigged**. For most training dinghies the following steps are involved:

1) Collect the sails, rudder, tiller, daggerboard and safety equipment for the particular boat you'll be using.

2) Prepare the hull

3) Position the boat so its bow points into the wind.

4) Rig the sails

5) Check that the required safety equipment is aboard.

If you learn the rigging procedure correctly and always do each step in order, you'll soon be able to rig a boat very quickly and still not forget anything. Let's take these steps one at a time:

Step 1 - Collecting the Parts

Usually sails, rudders, tillers and daggerboards are stored under cover to protect against weather damage and theft. Gather up these parts and carry them to the dinghy you'll be using. If the boat and its parts are numbered, check that the numbers match.

Step 2 - Preparing the Hull

Procedures vary from one type of training boat to another. The important thing is to learn a sequence and stick to it. If you're rigging in the water, the first thing you'll need to do is get aboard. Carefully step into the centre of the cockpit and crouch down right away. Never jump into a boat, or step onto the **gunwale** (outer edge of the hull).

While rigging on shore, try to work from outside the boat as much as possible. Small kids may need to climb aboard to reach some of the parts, but a heavier person could damage the hull.

With any boat stored on shore, check for water sloshing around inside the hull and drain it if necessary. Then screw in the **drain plug** (usually located near the bottom of the transom). If there's a **suction bailer** in the cockpit, check that it's closed.

Most training dinghies are stored with their masts upright and mainsheets led through their blocks, but if these items need to be rigged, your instructor will show you how.

In most cases, the only other steps in preparing the hull are attaching the rudder-tiller, and inserting the daggerboard or lowering the centreboard. Depending upon the kind of boat and whether you're rigging on shore or in the water, you may need to put off some of these steps until after the sails are up and you're getting under way. Again, your instructor can help you decide the right method.

Step 3 - Facing the Boat Upwind

Unless you point the bow into the wind when you rig the sails, they can blow over the side or even tip the boat. If the boat is sitting on a launching dolly or trailer, simply wheel it around so it faces into the wind. When rigged in the water alongside a dock, tie the boat to the downwind side of the dock using only the **painter** (bow line). This way, the boat will swing to point into the wind while you work.

Diagram 9) Rigging while tied to a dock.
Hanks (inset) attach the jib to the forestay.

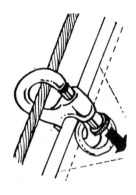

Step 4 - Rigging the Sails

A bagged sail makes a nice, neat package, but a sail on the loose can be pretty unruly. Wait until you're ready to rig a sail before removing it from the sail bag. Then unfold it carefully to avoid a mess. Two sailors working together can save time, if one rigs the mainsail while the other rigs the jib.

To rig the mainsail, begin by locating the **clew** (lower rear corner) of the mainsail. On most boats the **foot** (bottom edge) of the mainsail slides into a groove running along the top of the boom. Feed the foot into the groove until the clew is almost at the end of the boom. Attach it to the **outhaul** either by tying a **bowline knot** through the clew with the outhaul or attaching the shackle on the end of the outhaul to the clew. On boats without a groove on the boom simply attach the clew to the outhaul line and tighten.

Next, pin or shackle the **tack** (lower front corner) of the mainsail to the front end of the boom. Then take the **luff** (front edge) of the mainsail and run your hand along the length until you reach the **head** (top corner) of the sail. This insures the sail isn't twisted.

Now, locate the **main halyard**, a line which passes through a block at the top of the mast and down again. Open the **shackle** that's fastened to one end of the main halyard and attach it to the head of the sail. Slide the sail into the groove in the mast just above the **gooseneck** (the fitting that attaches the boom to the mast) and pull the main halyard until it is tight and the head of the sail has been raised about one foot. Cleat the halyard so it won't slip back again.

Diagram 10) Sail parts and rigging details.

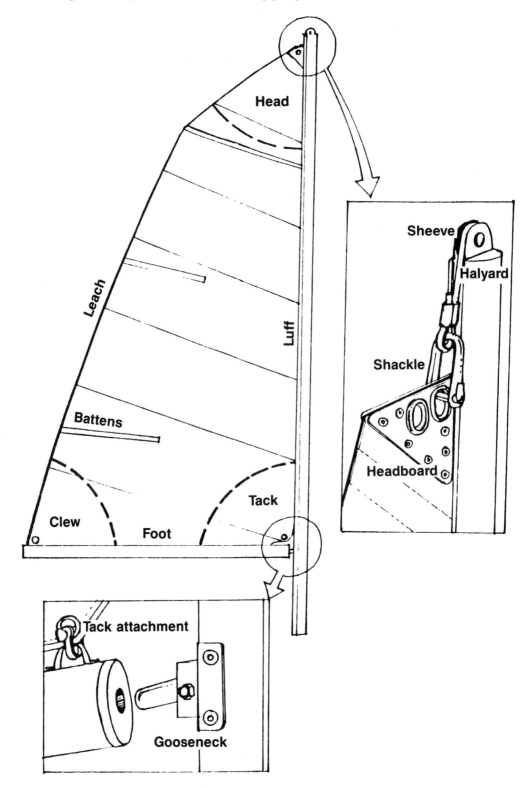

Head

Leach

Luff

Battens

Clew

Foot

Tack

Sheeve

Halyard

Shackle

Headboard

Tack attachment

Gooseneck

If your training boat has removeable **battens** to help support the **leech** (rear edge) of its mainsail, this is the time to slip them into the batten pockets. The mainsail is now ready to hoist.

To rig the jib, remove it from the sail bag and attach its tack to the appropriate fitting near the bottom of the **forestay**. Usually the luff of the jib is secured to the forestay using little clips along the luff called **hanks**, so work your way up the luff attaching the hanks one at a time. After the jib is hanked on, shackle the jib halyard to the head of the jib.

The jib sheets of most training dinghies are permanently attached to the **cringle** (metal ring) at the clew of this sail, and are stored along with the sail in the sail bag. To rig the jib sheets, just thread each one through one of the jib fairleads located on each side of the cockpit. Use **Figure 8 Knots** (see next page) to prevent the jib sheets and mainsheet from coming out of the blocks or fairleads while you're sailing.

The final step in rigging the sails is to raise each sail by pulling downward on the loose end of its halyard. When the sail is hoisted fully, cleat the halyard and neatly coil the halyard tail so the sail can be dropped quickly if necessary. In some situations it's better to hoist the main first, while in others the jib should lead off — discuss this with your instructor.

Step 5 - Checking the Safety Gear

In addition to certifying PFDs, the Department of Transport publishes the Canadian Coast Guard's Safe Boating Guide (required reading for this course) which includes lists of required safety equipment for various types of boats. On a typical sail training dinghy, there should be two paddles, a bailer, and a whistle or horn, as well as the approved PFD for each sailor aboard. Double check that this gear is serviceable and properly secured.

Knots and Related Skills

Handling a sailboat means handling lines, so it really helps to learn a few knots and other "tricks of the trade".

A good knot is quick to tie, easy to untie, and above all, secure. Here are a few knots and line handling skills that you'll need to rig and sail a boat:

Diagram 11) Sailing knots

Figure 8 Knot - Used as a "stop knot" to prevent a line from sliding back through a block or fairlead.

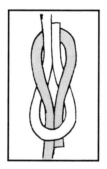

Reef Knot - Easily tied knot for joining two lines of the same size and type.

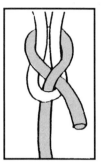

Sheet Bend - A knot for joining two lines of unequal thickness together. More reliable than the reef knot if the lines are slippery.

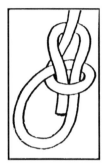

Bowline - Makes a loop at the end of a line that stays open instead of sliding closed like a noose. Used to tie the painter to the bow ring, for attaching sheets and halyards to sails, and for many other purposes.

Round Turn with Two Half Hitches - Used to tie a boat to a dock.

Cleat Hitch - Used to secure a line to a horn cleat.

Coiling Lines - To coil a line neatly, give the line a quarter twist each time you add another coil to the stack.

Diagram 12) Coiling lines

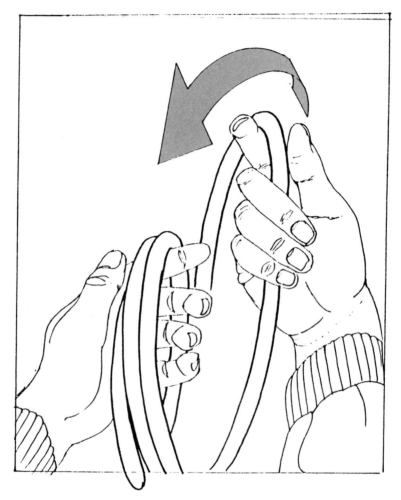

Chapter 8 — Out on the Water: First Skills

Key Ideas:
- Sailing Teamwork
- Getting Underway
- Tiller Steering Action
- Steering by the Sails
- Using Ticklers
- Slowing and Stopping

Every sport has its fundamental skills. The skills discussed in the next four chapters are the real foundation of sailing, just as skating is the basis of ice hockey. You will use them every time you go out in a sailboat.

Skipper-Crew Teamwork

Most sailing dinghies are handled by two sailors working in partnership. The **skipper** steers the boat, controls the mainsheet and is ultimately responsible for making sure that the boat is handled safely. While sailing, the skipper should sit on the windward side of the boat (opposite the boom) about even with the forward end of the tiller. If you always steer from this position, it's easier to see the sails, to sense changes in the wind, and to avoid becoming disoriented during maneuvers.

The **crew** balances the boat from side-to-side, keeps a lookout for other boats, and handles the jib (on sloops). In most dinghies, the crew sits just ahead of the skipper about even with the centreboard.

If the wind is light, the crew should sit on the leeward side of the boat (under the boom) to offset the weight of the skipper to windward. As the wind gets stronger, the crew will need to move further and further to windward to counteract the tipping force of the sails. These movements should be made smoothly to avoid shaking or jerking the boat. Remember, the crew's role is every bit as important as the skipper's. Both must communicate effectively and work cooperatively to handle a sailboat well.

Of course, if you're learning to sail **single handed**, you'll need to take on the jobs of both skipper and crew. At first this will seem like quite a handful, but before long it will start to feel natural. For beginners, the most difficult part of single handed sailing is steering and balancing the boat at the same time. If the wind is light, you may have to steer from the middle of the boat, crouched under the boom.

Diagram 13) Steering a single hander in light winds can be awkward.

Getting Underway

When a sailboat starts up from a stand still, it's called **getting underway**. Once you have the boat ready to sail (rigged and launched with crew and skipper aboard) the basic idea is very simple:

Ready - Ease all sheets completely and turn the boat so it's pointing toward open water with the wind blowing across the hull from one side. The **boom** will swing out in line with the wind, while the sail (or sails) flaps.

Set - Skipper and crew get into their sailing positions: Skipper sits facing the boom with rear hand on the tiller ready to steer. Crew pushes off, then balances the boat.

Go - Skipper pulls in the mainsheet until the sail stops flapping and fills. If the boat has a jib, the crew pulls in the leeward jib sheet at the same time. As the boat starts to move, the crew may need to sit to windward to prevent tipping.

Diagram 14) Getting underway.

Ready
- Ease sheets so sails flap

Set
- Crew pushes off. Skipper gets ready to steer.

Go
- Sheet in and balance the boat.

As you can see, actually getting the boat underway is no big deal. However, **getting ready** to get underway can be a bit more complicated. Chapter 16 will discuss how to handle the trickier "takeoffs" and "landings". But while you're first starting to sail, chances are you'll either be launching off a beach or departing from the downwind side of a dock. Here's what's involved:

Launching off a Beach or Ramp

Step 1 - Rig boat and hoist sails on shore, but keep the centreboard and rudder blade retracted so they won't scrape on the ground. Check that main and jib sheets are completely eased.

Step 2 - Wheel or carry the boat into thigh deep water keeping the bow pointed into the wind as much as possible.

Step 3 - Lower the centreboard or daggerboard part way and mount the rudder or lower its blade.

Step 4 - While crew (or helpers) steady the boat, skipper climbs aboard and gets into proper sailing position ready to steer.

Step 5 - Crew (or helpers) turn the boat sideways to the wind with the bow pointed away from shore.

Step 6 - Crew climbs aboard and gets into sailing position.

Step 7 - Sheet in and go, as described above.

Step 8 - As soon as the water is deep enough, crew lowers the centerboard all the way. This makes the boat less tippy.

Getting Underway from a Dock

Step 1 - Rig boat fully (sails up) as discussed in Chapter 6. Since the boat is already floating in deep water, the rudder should be mounted and the centreboard completely down. Main and jib sheets should be fully eased, so the sails flap freely.

Step 2 - Pull the painter to bring the boat up to the dock and turn it so the bow points toward open water.

Step 3 - Crew steadies the boat while the skipper steps gently into the centre of the cockpit and sits down.

Step 4 - Skipper reaches out to hold the boat alongside the dock while the crew unties the painter. Crew then steps aboard and sits near the centre of the boat in front of the skipper.

Step 5 - Crew pushes the boat away from the dock, turning it a little, if necessary, so that the wind is blowing directly across the hull.

Step 6 - Sheet in and go, as described above.

Steering With the Tiller

A moving bike or car will turn the same direction as you turn the handlebars or steering wheel, but a sailing dinghy is different. When you move the tiller to one side the boat turns toward the other way! This may feel strange at first, but you'll soon get the hang of it. Here are a few tips:

Diagram 15) Correct steering position

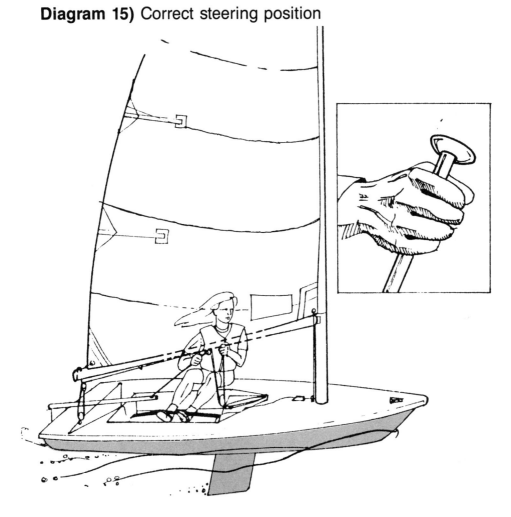

Steering Position - Sit comfortably on the windward side of the boat, facing to leeward, rear hand on the tiller or tiller extension, and forward hand holding the mainsheet.

Using a Tiller Extension - The tiller extension should angle forward and upward across your chest. Hold it using an overhand grip with your thumb pointing toward the end of the extension. Sailors often call this the **microphone grip** because it resembles the way rock stars hold their mikes.

Just as a bike or car won't turn when it's standing still, a sailboat won't respond to movements of the tiller unless its underway. The faster it goes, the better it steers. Remember, its important to get the boat moving first before trying to steer with the tiller.

How to Steer Using Clues from the Sails

The course or path of a sailboat is often related to the direction of the wind. Moving the tiller toward the mainsail will turn the bow of the boat toward the source of the wind. This is called **heading up**. Moving the tiller away from the sail will swing the bow away from the wind. This is **heading down** or **bearing off**.

After sheeting in and getting the boat underway, try heading up by gently moving the tiller toward the sail. If you do this without adjusting the sheets, the sail will begin to flap again like it did before you got underway. When this happens, gently move the tiller away from the sail until the boat begins to head down.

As the boat heads down, watch for the moment that the sail stops flapping and re-fills. Try to stop your turn away from the wind at the moment the sail fills completely, and the boat will pick up speed.

When you steer this way, taking your clues from the sails, the boat will follow a path that is slightly wiggly. Each time you see that the sails are completely full, head up gradually while watching the luff or front portions of the sails. As soon as the luff area begins to flutter a little, it's your signal to start heading down until the fluttering stops.

Diagram 16) Steering by watching the sails:

Head down when they flutter,
head up when they don't.

Steering with the Help of Ticklers

Ticklers are short pieces of yarn taped to the two sides of a sail a short distance behind the luff. Ticklers make it easier to steer by the sails because they will quickly alert you, not only when you need to head down, but also when you need to head up or are already right on course.

Diagram 17) Steering by the Ticklers:

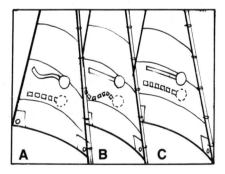

A) *Windward tickler flutters* — head down.
B) *Leeward tickler flutters* — head up.
C) *Both ticklers streaming* — just right!

In to Go and Out to Slow

Heading up so that the sails flap is one way to slow down in a sailboat. The other is the opposite of what you do when you sheet in to get underway: just release the sheets to "let the wind out of your sails" while steering straight ahead.

Diagram 18) Two Ways to Stop

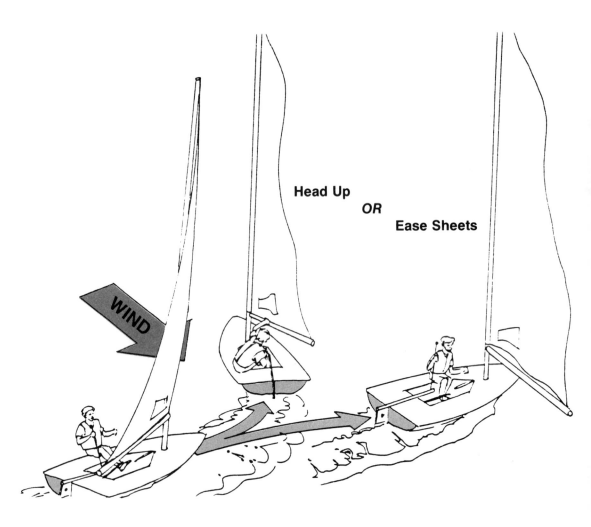

Both ways, what you're doing is shutting off the power so the boat will lose speed. If the sails flap long enough the boat will coast to a halt. But don't forget that a sailboat has no brakes and can't stop "on a dime".

To get a feel for how much space is needed for your boat to coast to a stop with its sails flapping, try a series of stops and starts. You can remember how to handle the main and jib sheets during this drill with the phrase: *in to go and out to slow*.

When the Wind Tips the Boat

When a gust of wind suddenly strikes the sail, it's natural for a sailboat to tip or **heel**. This is OK as long as it doesn't get out of hand, but it's important to know how to keep heel under control. The trick is to head up a little or ease the sheets a little whenever the boat begins to tip too much. The idea is exactly the same as stopping the boat, but you won't need to flutter the sails as much or as long.

Diagram 19) Head up if the wind starts to tip the boat too much.

Chapter 9 — Basic Sail Adjustments

Key Ideas:
- Playing the Sail
- Turn the Boat or Trim Its Sails
- If in Doubt, Sheet Out
- Sailing Higher, Sailing Lower
- Steering a Straight Course
- Main and Jib Together

At the end of the last chapter, you learned two different ways to stop a moving sailboat. The first is to use the tiller to turn the bow of the boat into the wind until the sails flap. The second is to let out the sheets until the sails flap. From a sail's point of view, these two actions are exactly the same. In both cases, the sail falls into line with the flow of wind. The only real difference is the orientation of the hull beneath the sail.

In the preceding chapter, you also learned to start a boat moving from a standstill by sheeting in until the sails stopped flapping. If your boat is already sailing along, you can use the same idea to **play the sail** so it's always set at the proper angle to the wind. To play a sail, you alternately sheet out until it begins to flutter a little near the luff, then sheet in until the fluttering stops. The action is a bit like playing a hooked fish because a good fisherman alternately lets out line (when the fish pulls hard) and reels back in (when it doesn't).

From a sail's viewpoint, playing the sail is just like the wiggly steering you learned in the last chapter because both are ways to find the proper angle between the sail and the wind. Steering does this by turning the whole boat including the sail. Playing the sail does it by changing just the angle of the sail while the boat's hull continues to travel straight ahead.

Diagram 20) Turn the boat or adjust the sail: two ways to find the correct angle between sails and wind.

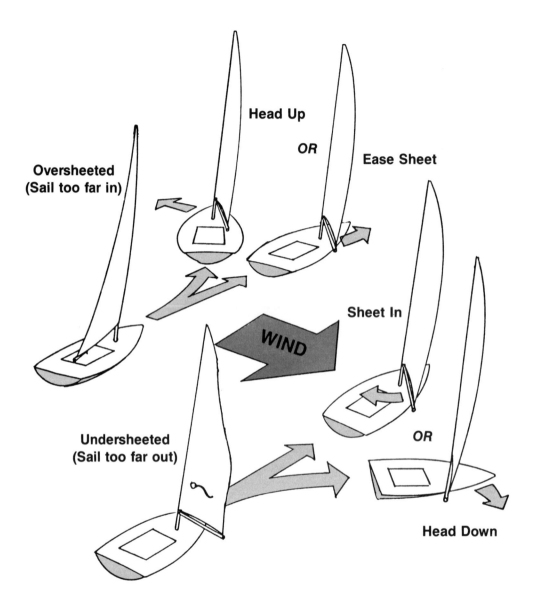

If in Doubt, Sheet Out

Playing the sail is a key part of **sail trimming** — keeping the sails correctly adjusted to the wind regardless of the direction the hull is pointing. It's not difficult to see when a sail is **undersheeted** because the luff area will start to flutter. But without tickers, it's harder to tell when a sail is **oversheeted**, since there's no change in the sail's appearance to let you know that it's time to sheet out. The only difference you may notice is that the boat will lose some speed.

Because the wind direction changes almost constantly while sailing, you need to frequently check to be sure that a nice, full-looking sail isn't really an oversheeted one. This is where playing the sail comes in: just ease out the sheet until you see the first signs of fluttering along the luff, then sheet in again until the fluttering goes away. The basic rule of sail trimming without ticklers is: **If in doubt, sheet out**. This is also a good rule to remember if an excess of wind in the sails is causing the boat to tip.

Sail Trimming with Ticklers

Yarn ticklers on a sail act like a kind of early warning system to let you know when the sail is either oversheeted or undersheeted. If the ticklers on the windward side of the sail start to lift and dance, sheet in slightly. If the ticklers on the leeward side start to flutter or droop, ease out some sheet. When both sets of ticklers are streaming back, Congratulations ! You've got the sail trimmed just right.

Sailing Higher and Lower Courses

Quite often in sailing you will want to steer in a particular direction rather than steering by the wind. Now that you understand the basics of sail trim you can start to do this by simply aiming the boat in the direction you want to go, then trimming the sails accordingly.

Let's say you're sailing along and you decide you want to head up so that the course of the boat angles closer to the wind. No problem, just say "**Heading Up**" (if you're sailing with a crew) and gently push the tiller toward the sail until the boat is pointing the way you want to go. Sheet in the sail (or sails) until they are once again trimmed correctly and you're on your way. Because you headed up when you changed from the old course to the new one, you are now said to be sailing a **higher** course.

Diagram 21) Heading up and heading down.

The sail should remain at the same angle
to the wind regardless of the course.

Learning to Steer a Straight Course

Bikes and cars go straight ahead unless deliberately steered into
a turn. Not so with sailboats. At first, it may seem like your boat
is always trying to veer away to one side or the other. The easiest
way to steer in a straight line is to look past the bow to a landmark
on the shore ahead. Whenever the boat begins to veer off course,
you'll see the bow begin to swing with respect to the landmark,
alerting you right away that it's time to make a small helm
adjustment.

Trimming Main and Jib Together

The skipper and crew aren't the only team on a sloop-rigged boat. Mainsail and jib are partners too. To drive the boat efficiently, the two sails need to be trimmed so that they work together. Here's how:

Step 1 - With the boat sailing on course, the crew adjusts the jib sheet in or out so that the ticklers on both sides are streaming back and the luff area of the jib is almost, but not quite fluttering.

Step 2 - The skipper switches from sailing a straight course to sailing by the jib, heading up or down as necessary to keep both sets of ticklers streaming back smoothly.

Step 3 - Now the skipper trims the mainsail, sheeting in or out until the mainsail luff begins to flutter whenever the windward jib ticklers start to lift and dance. The two sails are now working in tandem.

Sail Trimming Tips:
- Trim the jib first, then the mainsail.
- Because the wind angle is always changing, both sails will need frequent re-trimming. Play the sails.
- Usually its easiest to trim the jib by using the jib ticklers, but to trim the main watch for slight signs of fluttering near its luff.

Chapter 10 - Learning to Come About

Key Ideas:
- Head Up and Sheet In
- The "No Go" Zone
- Skipper's Moves
- Crew's Moves
- Caught in Irons

After you've sailed away from dock or shore for a while, you'll want to turn around and head back. Here's the basic steps for **coming about**:

Step 1 - Preparation: Skipper alerts crew of intention to come about with the command "**Ready About**". When set to go the crew replies "**Ready**".

Step 2 - Heading Up: Skipper says "**Helm's a-Lee**" , moves the tiller toward the sail to head up, and simultaneously sheets in the mainsail. On sloop-rigged dinghies, crew sheets in the jib.

Step 3 - Bow-to-Wind: Skipper holds the tiller over to keep the boat turning steadily past the point where the sails start to flap and past the point where the bow of the boat is pointing directly upwind. As the boat turns through the bow-to-wind position, the skipper moves to the opposite side of the boat and switches hands so the aft hand is once again steering and the forward hand is handling the mainsheet.

On a sloop, the crew releases the old jib sheet at the bow-to-wind position and reaches over to pull in the jib sheet on the other side, while shifting body weight as needed to balance the boat.

Step 4 - Heading Down: Skipper allows the boat to continue turning until the sails fill again, this time with the wind blowing over the other side.

Step 5 - Finishing Off: Skipper centers the tiller to stop the turn. Sail trim should be checked so boat will pick up speed quickly.

Diagram 22) Coming About

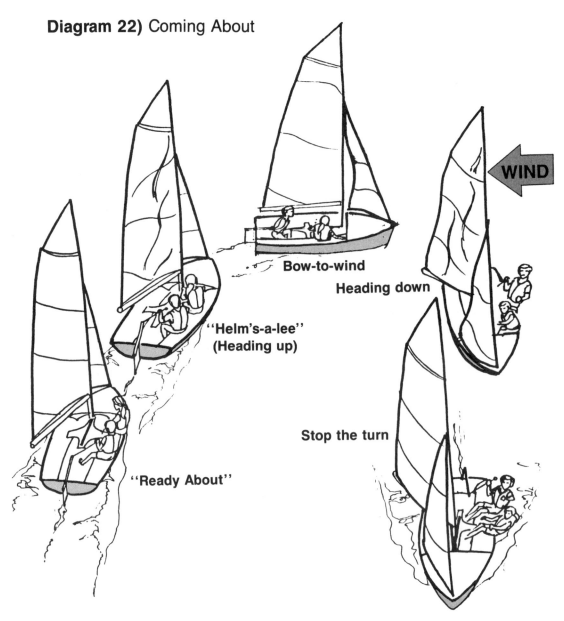

Bow-to-wind

Heading down

"Helm's-a-lee"
(Heading up)

WIND

Stop the turn

"Ready About"

Busting Through the "No Go Zone"

You probably noticed that the first step in coming about is exactly the same as turning the boat into the wind to make it stop. Any time a sailboat aims too close to upwind, its sails will flap and it will begin to slow to a halt.

With the sheets pulled in further, the boat will sail closer to the wind without the sails flapping, but there's a limit. For most dinghies, this limit is about 45 degrees from upwind. This means that to come about, a boat has to turn through 45 degrees with the sails flapping before it reaches the bow-to-wind position and another 45 degrees before the sails fill again on the other side. This 90 degrees sector in which the sails provide no power is sometimes called the **no-go zone**.

Here's a few things you can do to help your boat coast through the no-go zone without stopping:

1) Be sure the boat is moving quickly before heading up to come about.

2) Sheet in as the boat heads up to keep the sails working until the last possible moment.

3) Turn the boat quickly and steadily, but don't jam the tiller all the way over. Coming about in most dinghies should take from 3 to 5 seconds.

Skipper's Actions for Coming About

When you're new to sailing, coming about may seem very complicated, but with practice it becomes easy and natural. Let's look at the trickiest part of this maneuver: the smooth movement of the skipper from one side of the boat to the other. The six steps below are diagrammed on the following two pages.

Step 1 - Ready About: You should be sitting on the windward side steering with your aft hand and holding the mainsheet with your forward hand.

Step 2 - Heading Up: Push tiller toward sail and step into the centre of the boat with your aft foot. Hand on the tiller extension should lead the way.

Step 3 - Bow-to-Wind: As you step across the boat, pivot your body to face forward. Crouch down so the boom passes over your head!

Step 4 - Heading Down: Continue to pivot your body as you prepare to sit down on the new windward side. While your body turns, your tiller arm should reach around behind your back to continue steering.

Step 5 - Sail Re-fills: By the time the boat has headed down enough that the sail stops flapping, you should be sitting down and steering with one arm behind your back. This sounds awkward, but it works fine. Bring the hand holding the mainsheet back so it can grasp both sheet and tiller extension at the same time.

Step 6 - Finishing Off: Now your behind-the-back hand can release the tiller extension and take the mainsheet. Swing the tiller extension up and over your rear shoulder, and you're back to the normal steering position.

Diagram 23) Skipper's movements while coming about.
(Numbers refer to steps in text)

1

2

3

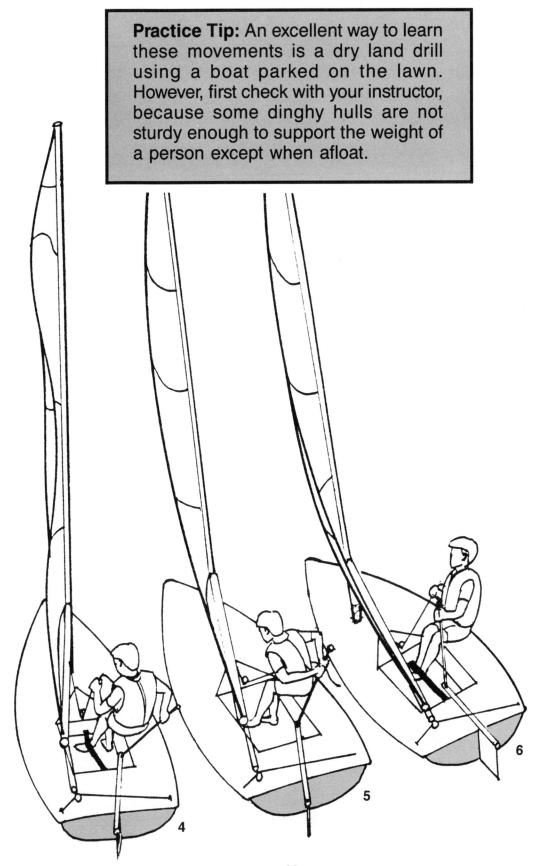

Practice Tip: An excellent way to learn these movements is a dry land drill using a boat parked on the lawn. However, first check with your instructor, because some dinghy hulls are not sturdy enough to support the weight of a person except when afloat.

Skipper's Hand Exchange Without a Tiller Extension

If there is no tiller extension, you should swap hands on the tiller behind your back as the boat comes bow-to-wind. At the moment of the exchange, reach your mainsheet hand (still holding the sheet) behind you to catch the tiller. With both the mainsheet and the tiller gripped in this hand, finish turning your body and sit down on the new windward side. Now reach for the mainsheet with your empty (forward) hand and go back to steering sailing as usual.

Crew's Actions Coming About

When a sloop-rigged boat comes about, the crew has three important jobs: First, checking that the boat won't run into anything when it changes course. Second, positioning body weight to keep the boat level while the skipper is busy changing sides, and third, handling the jib. For the crew, coming about should go like this:

Step 1 - Preparation for Coming About: At the skipper's command of "*Ready About*", you should check to be sure you're holding the leeward (working) jib sheet in your aft hand, and that you're prepared to move across the boat. You then reply "*Ready*" to let the skipper know its OK to come about. The skipper will say "*Helm's-a-lee*" and begin heading up.

Step 2 - Heading Up: If the jib is not already sheeted all the way in, smoothly bring it in the rest of the way. If it is held in a cam cleat, pop it out of the cleat by lifting the tail of the sheet and pulling.

Step 3 - Approaching Bow-to-Wind: As the jib begins to flap, shift your body toward the middle of the boat, and let the old jib sheet drop from your aft hand. Next, pick up the new jib sheet with the same hand so you won't have to reach back for it a moment later as you move across the boat.

Step 4 - Bow-to-Wind: Step over the centreboard trunk with your forward foot while pivoting your body so you face the stern of the boat. Remember to duck low, so the boom will clear your head.

Step 5 - Heading Down: Transfer the new jib sheet to your aft hand and pull in the jib as it begins to re-fill. At the same time, sit down on the new windward side. In strong winds, you may need to use both hands to sheet in the jib.

Getting Out of Irons

Getting **caught in irons** is an old time sailing phrase that describe what happens when a boat fails to finish coming about and slows to a stop in the No-Go zone. Once the boat is no longer underway, the tiller won't work, and it can be quite difficult to get the boat turned and underway again.

The quickest way to get out of irons is to push both the tiller and the boom in the direction you want the boat to turn. With sloops, it also helps for the crew to hold the jib out on the side opposite the boom.

If you take these steps, the boat will spin around as soon as the wind starts pushing it backward. When the wind is once again blowing across the hull from the side, just sheet in and sail away.

Diagram 24) Getting out of irons

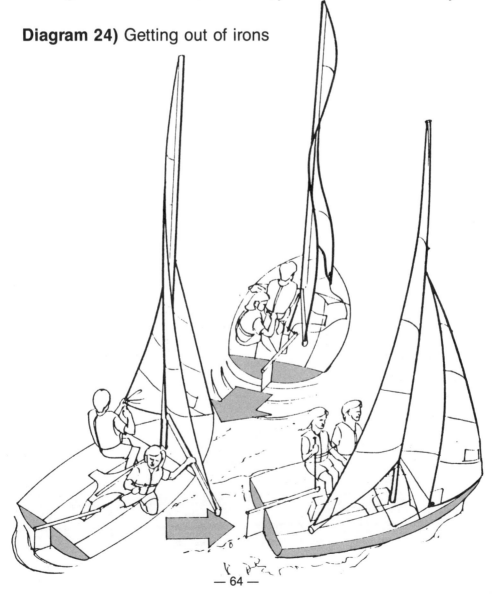

Chapter 11 — Learning to Gybe

Key Ideas:
- **The Gybe Path**
- **Crew's and Skipper's Actions**
- **Accidental Gybes and "Laser" Gybes**

To come about in a sailboat, you swing the bow into the wind and continue the turn until the sails fill again from the other side. To gybe, you head down instead of up, flipping the mainsail across the boat when the bow is pointing downwind.

Gybing is both easier and more challenging than coming about. It's easier because the wind is pushing the boat along throughout

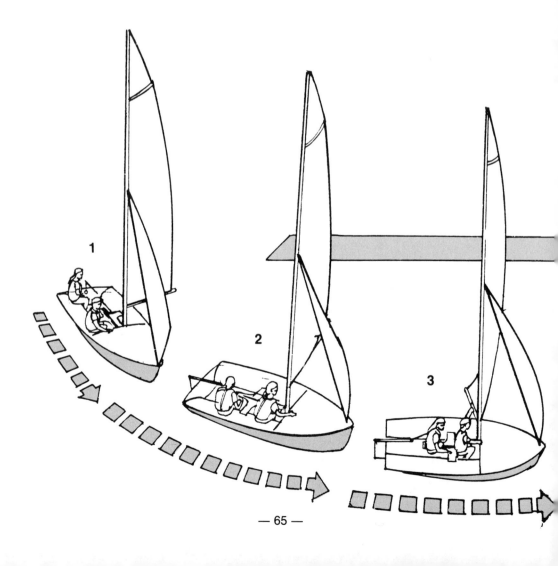

the maneuver making it impossible to get caught in irons along the way. It's more challenging because a gybe can get out of hand if done incorrectly in strong winds. In a gentle breeze, nothing can go seriously wrong while you're learning to gybe, so relax and enjoy yourself.

The Gybe Path

Steering the boat along the proper **gybe path** is a very important part of gybing correctly. The proper gybe path begins with a curve as the boat heads down, but straightens out momentarily as the skipper or crew flips the mainsail across the boat. Once the main is gybed, you can begin to head up with the wind on the other side of the boat.

Diagram 25) The gybe path.
(Numbers refer to steps on page 67.)

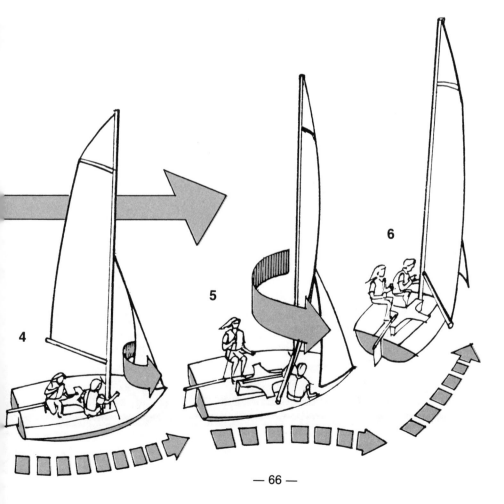

Gybing Details: Roles for Skipper and Crew

Step 1 - Skipper moves the tiller away from the sail a little to head down gradually. Sheets are eased out as the boat turns.

Step 2 - While continuing to slowly head down, skipper crosses the boat to sit on the leeward (boom) side and gives the warning "***Ready to Gybe***". Crew should reply "***Ready***" before proceeding to the gybe itself.

Step 3 - In a sloop, watch for the jib to go limp as the mainsail blocks it's wind — a sign that the boat is pointed directly downwind. Skipper should continue the slow turn beyond the downwind position. In most sloops, this will immediately cause the jib to flip across the boat — the signal for Step 4, the gybe itself.

Step 4 - Skipper gives the command "***Gybe Ho***". The crew (or in singled handed boats, the skipper) grabs the mainsheet or boom and tosses the mainsail across the boat. At the same time, the skipper briefly moves the tiller away from the direction that the boom is swinging to straighten the boat's course and keep it from heading up too fast after the gybe.

Step 5 - Crew drops the old jib sheet and picks up the new one. Once this is done, the skipper can give the command "Heading Up".

Step 6 - Head up gradually, sheeting in as the boat turns.

In addition to swinging the mainsail across the boat, the crew's jobs during a gybe are: looking out for other boats and obstacles, keeping the boat level, and handling the jib sheets.

Accidental Gybes and "Laser" Gybes

An accidental gybe will occur if the skipper keeps turning the boat far beyond a straight downwind course without remembering to flip the mainsail across. If you make this mistake, the time will come when the wind suddenly fills the mainsail from the "wrong" side and flings it across the boat. If this happens in strong winds it may damage the boat or cause a capsize, but when the wind is light, it does no real harm.

If you're learning to sail in a Laser, the correct way to gybe is somewhat like an accidental gybe — you've got to keep turning slowly until the wind catches behind the mainsail and flings it across. The three keys to maintaining control while gybing a Laser are to switch sides (and steering hands) before the gybe occurs, to quickly jerk in some mainsheet shortly before the gybe, and to steer the boat in the direction the boom is swinging during the gybe itself.

Chapter 12 — Back to Shore

Key Ideas:
- **Slow and Easy**
- **Dock Landings**
- **Beach Landings**
- **De-rigging**
- **Sail care**

Pilots say that landing is the trickiest part of flying an airplane, and bringing a sailboat into the dock or beach is also more challenging that sailing around in open water. Of course, a crash landing in an airplane is likely to be more serious than in a sailboat, but in either case, it's very important to learn how to land right.

The basic rule for approaching a dock or beach is **come in slowly**. Remember, a sailboat won't slow down unless the bow is pointed into the wind enough that the sails can flap. This means that a controlled approach can only be made when the wind is blowing across the boat and there is space to windward so you can head up as necessary.

Dock Landings

Unless there are too many other boats there already, coming in to the leeward side of a dock is by far the easiest way to land a sailboat. Windward side dock landings are another story and should not be attempted until you have more sailing experience under your belt (see Chapter 16).

Here are the steps involved in a normal landing on the leeward side of a dock:

Step 1 - Identify the leeward side and select the spot where you wish to land.

Step 2 - Position your boat for a "hooked" or J-shaped approach. Plan to arrive about a boat's length to leeward of the target spot, so you'll have enough space to turn into the wind and bring the boat to a controlled stop.

Step 3 - Make your initial approach with the wind blowing across the boat. You can alternately sheet in and sheet out as you get close to reduce and control speed. In a really good landing the boat will come to a complete stop about an arm's length from the target spot.

Step 4 - Secure the boat to the dock using the painter. Skipper and crew climb out one at a time, or proceed with de-rigging.

Diagram 26) Dock landings:
The right way and the wrong way.

YES — Target spot to windward, sails fluttering to lose speed.

NO — Aiming downwind, no way to stop.

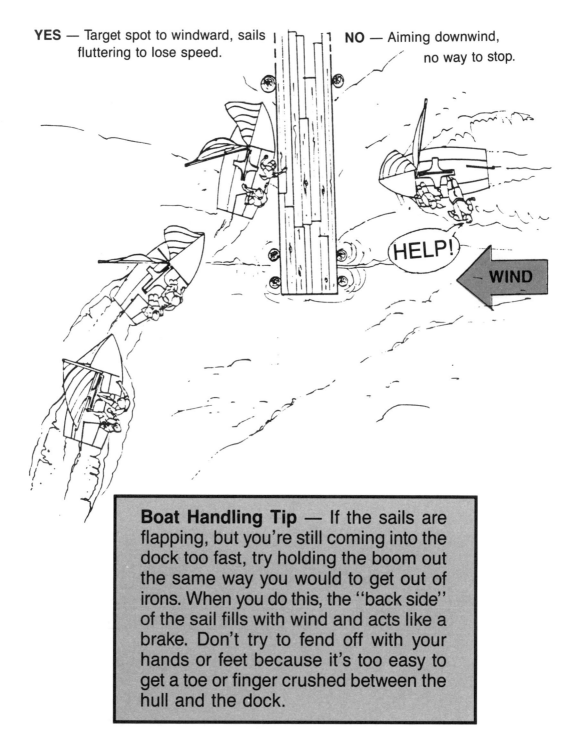

Boat Handling Tip — If the sails are flapping, but you're still coming into the dock too fast, try holding the boom out the same way you would to get out of irons. When you do this, the "back side" of the sail fills with wind and acts like a brake. Don't try to fend off with your hands or feet because it's too easy to get a toe or finger crushed between the hull and the dock.

Beach Landings

Landing on a beach or launching ramp is usually quite easy unless there are strong winds and large waves — conditions you probably won't need to deal with at this early stage in your sailing career. A wind blowing directly toward shore presents some special problems that are discussed in Chapter 16 (p. 84). For now, let's assume that the wind is blowing along the shore or from the land.

Step 1) Select an approach path to the beach that will have the wind blowing across the boat from the side along the way. If possible you should allow space to head up almost bow-to-wind when you reach the shallow water near shore.

Step 2) Make your approach, alternately sheeting in and sheeting out to limit your speed.

Step 3) Ease the sheets completely and just before the water gets too shallow, raise the centreboard or lift the daggerboard out of it's slot and lay it down inside the boat. If necessary, raise the rudder also (ask your instructor about this).

Step 4) Allow the boat to coast into the shallows with sails flapping. While the skipper balances the boat, the crew should step out and stand on the bottom. Crew then steadies the boat while the skipper steps out.

Step 5) Skipper raises or removes rudder. Then skipper and crew either carry the boat out of the water, or wheel a launching cart into the water and slide the boat onto the cart. Dinghies should *never* be dragged up a beach !

Diagram 27) Beach landing with the wind along the shore

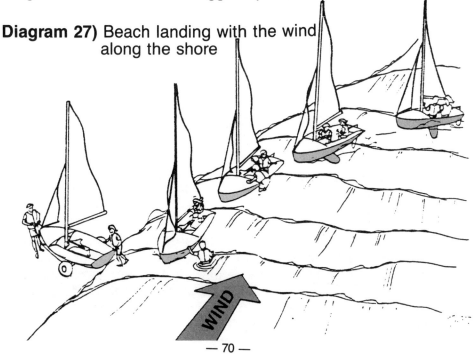

WIND

Putting the Boat to Bed

Ordinarily, a boat is de-rigged in the reverse order of rigging. Once the sails are off and the hull de-rigged, remove the drain plug in the transom and raise the bow so any water inside can run out. If you sail in salt water, it's a good idea to hose off the boat and its fittings to help minimize corrosion.

Sail Care

If the sails are wet with salt water they should be rinsed and dried if possible before storage. This can often be done by wheeling the fully rigged boat over to a faucet and hosing it down.

Sails can also be dried on a flat, clean surface such as a lawn. When dry, they should be folded in a zigzag fashion by two people working together. Start at the foot and fold the sail back and forth like a road map so that each fold stacks on top of the last. Then roll or fold up the whole stack starting at the luff.

Diagram 28) Sail folding

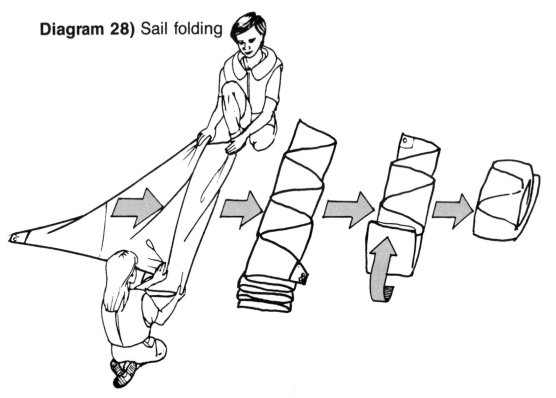

If the mainsail has removeable battens, take them out before folding. If the battens are sewn in, you'll have to be sure that the leech of the mainsail stays in a straight line with each fold. By making each fold a little wider at the leach than the luff, you can keep the leech (and battens) in line, so the sail will fit into the bag once its folded from luff to leach.

Chapter 13 — Going Places by Sailboat

Key Ideas:
- **Running Before the Wind**
- **Broad Reach**
- **Beam Reach**
- **Close Reach**
- **Close Hauled**
- **Port and Starboard Tack**
- **Alternate Terminology**

Until now in your sail training program, you've probably been zooming around without trying to go anywhere in particular, except when it's time to head in for a landing. But often sailors have a particular destination in mind when they set out. Now that you've mastered some fundamental sailing skills, it's time to learn how to go travelling in a sailboat.

The strength and direction of the wind is obviously very important when travelling by sail, but by maneuvering the boat properly, you can go almost anywhere on the water — even to a destination that's directly upwind. As the diagram below shows, it's all a matter of how you steer, trim your sails, and handle your boat.

Diagram 29) Points of sail

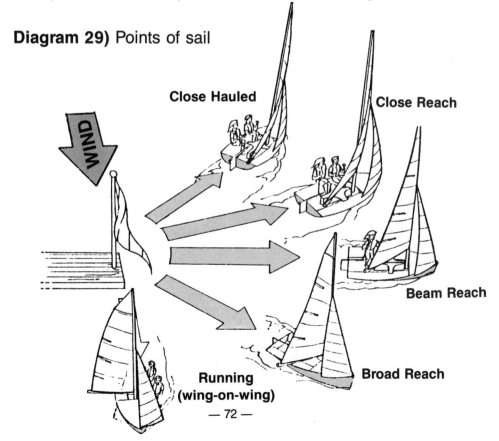

Close Hauled

Close Reach

WIND

Beam Reach

Running
(wing-on-wing)

Broad Reach

Depending upon the angle between the course and the wind, a moving sailboat is always on one of the five **Points of Sail** as shown on the diagram. It's sometimes suggested that the No-Go zone (closer to upwind than **close hauled**) is a sixth point of sail, but this is questionable, since a boat can only head up into the No-Go zone for a few seconds at a time.

Running before the wind, as the name implies, is sailing directly downwind like a floating ball in a pond. When running, the boat is travelling in the same direction as the wind, so you feel less wind than on other points of sail. The sheets should be eased out as much as possible. Downwind, the yarn ticklers all droop and are useless for sail trim. The mainsail will block wind from reaching the jib unless the jib is flipped over to the side opposite the boom — a move known as **winging the jib** or sailing **wing on wing**.

To shift from a run to a **broad reach**, the skipper heads up a few degrees. In most cases the boat will gain speed slightly and the jib of a sloop will begin to fill properly on the same side as the main. Sheets should be eased almost all the way. The ticklers still won't help you to trim the sails, but the watching for slight fluttering near the luffs may work.

On a **beam reach**, the wind is blowing directly across the **beam** or width of the boat's hull. In heading up from a broad reach to a beam reach, it's necessary to sheet in to maintain proper sail trim. Sail ticklers now work fine to indicate when sheet adjustments are required. When beam reaching, you feel the wind more than on a broad reach or a run because you are no longer moving away from it.

By heading up a few degrees more, the beam reach becomes a **close reach**. The feeling of wind on your face is stronger because the boat now angles into the wind.

Heading up and sheeting in even more puts the boat on a **close hauled** course. This really means that the sheets are hauled in as close (tightly) as is helpful when travelling towards an upwind destination. Sailing close hauled, you feel the wind strongly because the boat's own speed is added to the natural speed of the wind.

Port Tack, Starboard Tack

On it's way to an upwind destination, a boat must sail close hauled, with the wind blowing first over one side and then over the other. When the starboard side of the boat is to windward, the boat is said to be on **starboard tack**. Likewise, when the wind is blowing over the port side, the boat is on **port tack**. Changing tacks by coming about is often called **tacking**.

The terms port tack and starboard tack apply, not only to close hauled boats, but to any point of sail. The two boats converging in the diagram are both beam reaching, but one is on starboard tack and the other on port. It's a basic sailing safety rule that starboard tack has right of way over port, so the port tack boat must change course to avoid the starboard tack one.

Running before the wind, the side the boom is on determines port and starboard tacks. This means you can gybe from port tack to starboard (or starboard to port) without changing direction. Remember:

   Boom to Starboard = Port Tack
   Boom to Port = Starboard Tack

Diagram 30) Port and starboard tacks

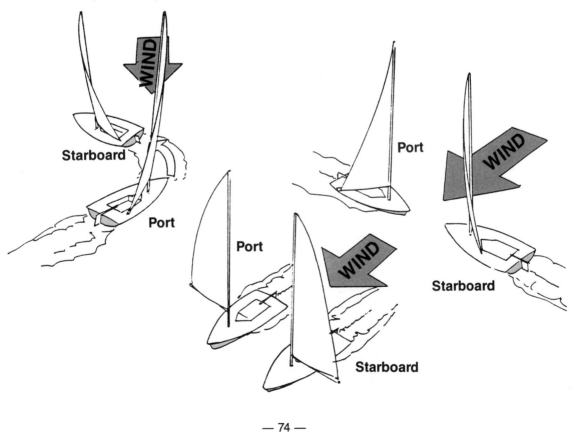

Sailors' Word Games

Because people have been sailing for centuries, sailors have come up with lots of different ways to say the same things. It's the same idea as using words like "leap", "spring" or "bound" as different ways of saying "jump".

As you go on in sailing, you'll hear more and more "alternative" sailing language. If you get confused, check the glossary at the back of this book or ask your instructor.

Some examples:

Sailing **close hauled** is also known as **sailing to weather, sailing upwind, hard on the wind, beating to windward,** or simply **beating**.

Heading down is the same thing as **bearing off** or **falling off**.

Now hold onto your seat, because the word games get even wilder. Besides using different terms to mean the same things, sailors often use one word to mean several different things. You've already seen how "**tack**"can refer to the lower front corner of a sail, the act of coming about, or to describe which side of the boat is windward (starboard or port).

The word "**luff**" is just as bad. So far in this book we've only used it to talk about the forward edge of a sail, but a sail can be said to luff when it flaps or flutters because it's undersheeted. Sailors also say that a boat luffs when it heads up. It seems awfully complicated, but at least when you've learned the jargon, then you too will be able to baffle and impress the **landlubbers**.

Chapter 14 — Upwind Sailing Skills

Key Ideas:
- Close hauled Trim
- Pinching and Footing
- Tacking Upwind
- Controlling Heel

Maneuvering your boat to an upwind destination is one of the most exciting and satisfying aspects of sailing. Although close hauled sailing is a lot like reaching, it requires more judgement and steering skill.

The boat in the diagram is properly set up for close hauled sailing. Skipper and crew are sitting close together on the windward side so their weight will offset the tendency of the boat to **heel** or tip. Both sails are sheeted fairly tightly (but not too tightly), and the boat is moving along quickly on a course about 45 degrees from the upwind direction. The skipper's steering is guided mainly by the ticklers on the jib as discussed in Chapter 9 . The centreboard is all the way down to minimize the tendency of the boat to skid sideways and to leeward.

Diagram 31) Correct trim for close hauled sailing

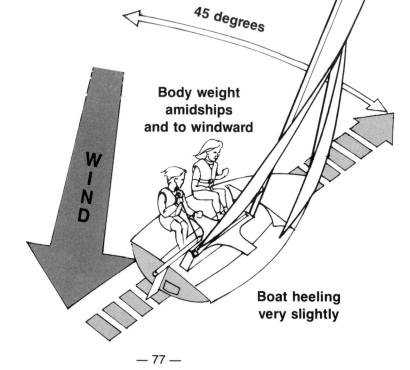

45 degrees

Body weight
amidships
and to windward

WIND

Boat heeling
very slightly

How Close to Haul?

Beginning sailors often wonder how tightly to sheet,and how much to head up for close hauled sailing. Obviously, if you really overdo it, you'll end up caught in irons in the No-Go zone. On the other hand, if you don't sheet in enough, the boat will go fast, but after a while you'll discover you've been close reaching back and forth without making much upwind progress. Trying to head up too much is called **pinching** and sailing below the correct close hauled course is called footing.

Diagram 32) Correct course for close hauled sailing.

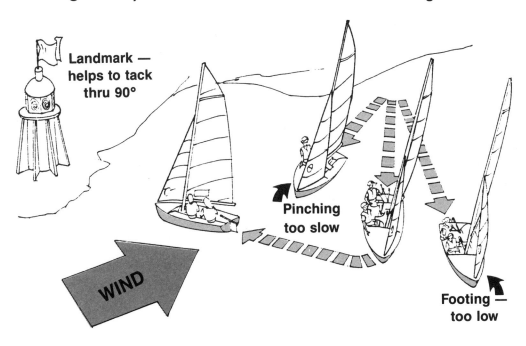

Landmark —
helps to tack
thru 90°

Pinching
too slow

WIND

Footing —
too low

When and How to Come About

If you're sailing to a nearby upwind destination, you may only need to tack once, but if you're going a long way to windward, it's often better to tack many times. For this reason, efficient tacking is an important part of upwind sailing skills.

When you first learned to come about (Chapter 10) you began the maneuver on a reaching course and sheeted in as you moved the tiller toward the sail. Sailing close hauled, the sheets are already in tight. To start the tack, all that you, as skipper, need to do is push the helm to leeward. If you're sailing with a crew, don't forget the warning command of "*Ready About*" followed by "*Helm's a-Lee*" after the crew has replied "*Ready*". These spoken communications remain very important, even after years of sailing experience.

New sailors often have problems judging how far to turn the boat during a tack. Turn too far and you'll end up on a close reaching course with the sails oversheeted. Not far enough and you're caught in irons.

A good way to avoid these problems is to select a landmark on shore to be your aiming point at the end of the tack. Look to windward over your shoulder to find a suitable landmark, then turn until the boat is pointed straight at the target. After a short while, you'll find that tacking becomes almost automatic and you'll no longer need to depend on landmarks.

Controlling Heel

The tendency of the wind force to heel (tip) a boat is greatest when sailing close hauled. Since most dinghies sail best if they are kept almost upright in the water, you will need to use body weight to minimize heel. Unless the wind is very light, both skipper and crew should sit side by side on the windward side of the hull.

As you gain confidence in your close hauled sailing, you can hook your feet under the **hiking straps** at the bottom of the cockpit and begin to **hike**, leaning your upper body backward to shift your weight even further to windward. But as always, the crew should stay ready to shift quickly toward the leeward side in case the boat begins to heel to windward.

Even with both crew to windward, the boat will sometimes start heeling too much. If this happens, just head up a little until the boat levels out. Sailing close hauled in strong winds, good skippers often ''pinch'' a little on purpose to keep the boat from heeling too much and slowing down. It also helps to ease the sheets slightly.

Diagram 33) Controlling Heel

Leeward heel — countered by sitting to windward and hiking (inset)

Windward heel — crew moves quickly to leeward.

Excess heel — countered by heading up.

Chapter 15 — Reaching and Downwind Skills

Key Ideas:
- Centreboard Adjustment
- Boom Vang
- Trim and Tiller Coordination
- Sailing Wing-on-Wing
- Sailing by the Lee
- The S-Gybe

Compared to upwind sailing, reaching and running probably seem simple — just aim the boat, trim the sails and go. All the same, there's plenty of room to develop skills which can make your cross wind and downwind sailing faster. smoother and more enjoyable. This chapter explains some reaching and downwind techniques that will prove very useful, especially as you begin to venture out in stronger winds.

Adjusting the Centreboard or Daggerboard

Up until now, you've always sailed with the centreboard all the way down except when leaving or entering the shallow water near a beach or launching ramp. Sailing close hauled, the centreboard should be fully extended to keep side-slipping or **leeway** to a minimum. But, if you head down to a beam reach, the tendency of the boat to skid sideways is greatly reduced making it OK to raise the centreboard about half way. Partially retracting the centreboard reduces drag, allowing the boat to go faster.

On a broad reach or when running before the wind, the centreboard can be raised even more — about 3/4 of the way. But it's better not to retract it completely because steering may become difficult (skidding in turns). Whenever the centreboard is up, the boat will become less stable, so if you're not feeling sure of yourself or start having control problems, just lower it again.

Using the Boom Vang

Most dinghies have an adjustable **boom vang** angling up from the base of the mast to the underside of the boom. Up until now, it's probably just been a nuisance — something that gets in the way during tacks and gybes. However, in stronger winds it stops the boom from lifting too much on reaches and runs. Keeping the boom vang snug (but not too tight) will make your mainsail work better and improve control during gybes.

Diagram 34) Using the boom vang

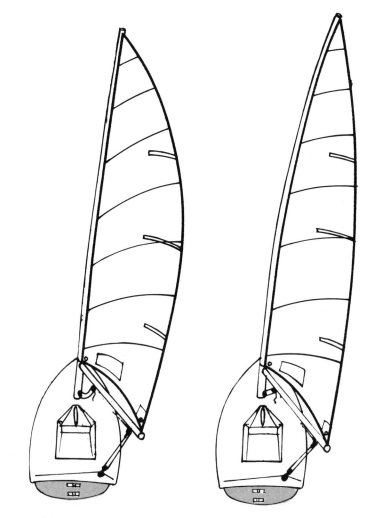

Slack vang allows too much mainsail twist on reaches and runs.

Tight vang reduces twist

Coordinating Trim and Tiller

Very often in sailing you want to change course by heading up or heading down. Although its perfectly possible to do so by first steering to the new course and later trimming the sails appropriately, you probably know by now that it's far more efficient to turn the boat and trim the sails at the same time. Skippers and crews should regularly practice trimming sails and steering in harmony using the commands "Heading Up" and "Bearing Off" to coordinate each course change. You'll soon find that sheeting the mainsail in helps the boat head up much more easily, while letting out the mainsheet encourages the boat to head down.

Diagram 35) Steering with the Sails

**Sheeting in the mainsail
helps head up.**

**Easing the mainsheet
helps head down.**

Sailing Wing-on-Wing

Running before the wind with the jib on the same side as the boom, the mainsail will block the flow of wind and make the jib limp. To keep the jib working, the crew can pull it across to the side opposite the boom and, if necessary, hold it out by hand. On some dinghies, a long stick called a **whisker pole** can be rigged to hold the clew of the jib away from the mast.

To keep the boat level while sailing wing-on-wing with the crew on the side opposite the boom, the skipper must cross the boat and sit beneath the boom. This is the same steering position that you learned for gybing in Chapter 11. As your sailing skills develop, it's a good idea to become accustomed to steering from the leeward (boom) side of the boat whenever you are broad reaching or running. This way, you're not only ready to gybe at any time, but getting used to the downwind steering position that's best for advanced sailing and spinnaker work.

Diagram 36) Setting the whisker pole

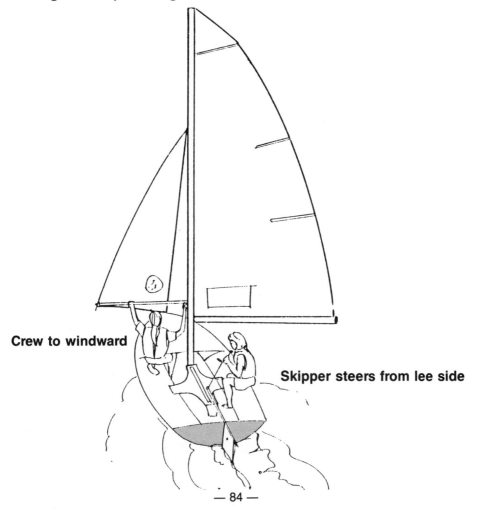

Crew to windward

Skipper steers from lee side

Sailing by the Lee

Running before the wind with the boom on the windward side of the boat is on is called SAILING BY THE LEE. A skilled skipper can deliberately sail by the lee and maintain control, but it's a poor idea in strong winds because of the increased risk of an accidental gybe (also known as a **crash gybe**, **c-gybe** or **slam gybe**).

Diagram 37) Sailing by the lee increases the risk of an accidental gybe.

On the other hand, it's good to practice some by-the-lee sailing in light winds. This drill teaches you what it feels like when the wind strays over to the "wrong" side of the stern — the same side as the mainsail. A masthead wind indicator or some yarn telltales tied to the shrouds are a big help in determining wind direction while sailing downwind.

Gybing in Stronger Winds

In Chapter 10 you learned to gybe by turning the boat from "reach to reach", reversing the helm briefly to straighten out the boat's course at the moment the mainsail gets flipped across. Now that you've learned to sail directly downwind, you've probably discovered that it's easy to gybe back and forth with little change of course.

Nevertheless, it's very important to practice moving the tiller opposite the direction the boom is swinging at the moment you flip the mainsail across. Sailors sometimes call this "steering the boat under the gybe". It's important because, in stronger winds, the boat tends to pivot quickly into the wind just after the mainsail is gybed. Unless you compensate by moving the tiller away from the direction the boom is swinging, the boat may **broach** (spin out) and perhaps capsize. The brief helm reversal at the moment of the gybe iself causes the boat to follow a slightly S-shaped course, so a well-managed gybe is often called an **S-gybe**.

Chapter 16 — Launching and Landing Challenges

Key Ideas:
- Beach Sailing in Onshore Winds
- The Upwind Side of a Dock
- Sailing from a Mooring

Sometimes it's a fine day for sailing, but the wind direction makes it difficult to get underway or return to shore. When this happens, some special know-how can make the difference between a great sail and a frustrating struggle or damaged boat.

Getting off the Beach in an Onshore Wind

In this situation, the wind and waves tend to push the boat back on the beach while you're trying to get underway. To make matters worse, you need to sail close hauled to get away from the beach into deep water, but the shallowness of the water near shore means that the centreboard can't be lowered very far.

Begin by pushing the boat out to water deep enough that the centreboard can be extended at least part way. With the sheets eased, turn the boat onto the tack that will get you into deep water most quickly. Then push off, climb aboard, skipper first, and sheet in quickly. Sail on a close reach (instead of close hauled) to get the boat moving quickly and minimize leeway. As the water depth increases, gradually let down the centreboard and extend the rudder blade.

Diagram 38) Off a beach against the wind.

Downwind Beach Landings

When the wind is blowing onshore, its often a good idea to lower the mainsail before coming into the beach to keep your speed under control. If the wind is light, it's OK to drop the main while broad reaching toward shore. But if the wind is strong, you should head up into the wind before lowering the main. Once the main is down it's easy to sail into the beach under good control using the jib alone.

Diagram 39) Beach landing in an onshore wind

WIND

To and From the Windward Side of a Dock

Sailors should avoid tying up to the windward sides of dock and floats because wind and waves tend to push and grind boats against them. But sometimes the wind swings around, or there's no space on the leeward side, so you need to know what to do.

If a boat must lie alongside the windward side of a dock, hang plastic fenders to protect the hull. Please don't use life jackets as fenders — they can easily be ruined.

Putting up the sails and trying to sail away from the windward side of a dock often won't work because the boat will be driven back to the side of the dock before it gets going. Instead, push off and paddle away with sails down. When a safe distance off, aim the boat into the wind and hoist the sails beginning with the main.

Landing on the windward side of a dock, use the same procedure in reverse. First, sail to a point upwind of the dock and drop the sails. Then drift downwind to the dock using your paddle to control or slow your approach if necessary.

Sailing from a Mooring

If the boat you're sailing is kept on a mooring, you'll need to learn to leave the mooring and return in safety. Leaving is easy. While still secured to the mooring, hoist the main followed by the jib. When you cast off from the mooring move the tiller in the direction that you wish to turn while pushing the boom out to the other side. It's really the same procedure used to escape when caught in irons.

Returning to a mooring is much the same as coming in to the leeward side of a dock. The idea is to head up with the sails flapping, controlling your speed so that the boat coasts to a stop with the bow alongside the mooring buoy in easy reach of the crew. If there is current sweeping you toward the buoy or away from it, you'll need to adjust the way you approach the mooring. If you've misjudged your speed and it looks like you'll overshoot the buoy, you may be able to stop the boat by backing the mainsail (as when getting out of irons). Otherwise, just head down, gybe and try again.

Chapter 17 — Capsize and Man Overboard

Key Ideas:
- Capsize Confidence
- Basic Recovery
- Scoop Recovery
- Walkover Recovery
- Righting a Turtled Boat
- Man Overboard Recovery
- Hypothermia Treatment

Capsizing is a normal part of small boat sailing — not a disaster that should be feared and avoided at all costs. If you sail too cautiously, your development as a sailor will be slowed; so it's best to try a few deliberate capsizes early in your sailing career so you can gain some confidence in your ability to right the boat. Be sure to practice self-righting in mild weather conditions, and only under your instructor's direct supervision.

Righting a Capsized Boat

Unless you're doing it for practice, capsize usually comes as a surprise — one moment you're sailing, the next you're in the "drink". Having been caught off guard, it's important to remember to stay calm as you go through the following steps:

Step 1 - Check that you're unhurt, holding onto the boat, and wearing your PFD properly. Then do a quick head count and verbal check to be sure that everyone else is also OK — not injured, tangled in a line, or trapped under the sails.

Step 2 - If any sheets are cleated, release them.

Step 3 - Check whether the bow of the capsized boat is facing the No-Go zone. If not, one sailor should grasp the bow and swim it around, so the wind doesn't fill the sails and tip the boat over again as soon as it's righted.

Step 4 - Move around the bottom of the capsized boat to reach the centreboard slot. Grab the end of the centreboard and extend it all the way.

Step 5 - Climb onto the end of the board, hold the edge of the hull with your hands, and lean back to right the boat. If skipper and crew are small, both may need to stand on the centreboard together to lift the rig out of the water. Be sure to drop back into the water as the boat swings upright because if you try to heave yourself aboard, your weight on the gunnel will probably capsize it to the opposite side.

Step 6 - After the boat is upright, climb aboard one at a time over the transom. If necessary, bail water out of the cockpit.

Diagram 40) Righting a capsized dinghy

These five steps represent a basic capsize recovery, but there are many variations. Provided one crew member is heavy enough to right the boat alone, you may be able to use a **Scoop Recovery** to bring the boat upright with the other crew already aboard. To perform a scoop recovery, the bigger crew member stands on the centreboard while the smaller crew member lies in the water holding onto a hiking strap. As the boat swings upright, the smaller crew member gets scooped into cockpit, ready to balance the boat and later, to help the larger crew member back aboard.

On some single handed dinghies such as the Laser, you can capsize and right the boat again without even getting wet! It's done by stepping over the rail and onto the centerboard as the boat capsizes; then stepping back over the rail and into the cockpit as the boat swings upright. Sailors call this nifty technique a **Walk-over Recovery** or **Dry Dunk**. Ask your instructor if it will work for the boat you're using.

Diagram 41) Walk over recovery

Turning Turtle and What to Do About It

If not righted, most dinghies will lie on their sides for quite a while with the mast and sails just under water. However, as the mast gradually floods or if someone tries to climb out of the water and onto the hull, the boat may eventually turn bottom up.

Righting a **turtled** or inverted boat can be very difficult, so it's best not to delay before recovering from a capsize. However, if you've waited too long, begin by tossing a jib sheet over the bottom of the hull. Next, climb on the bottom and lean back against the jib sheet to gradually bring the mast back up to the horizontal or capsized position. At this stage, extend, the centreboard and do your normal capsize recovery.

If you think the mast tip may be stuck in the bottom, proceed with great caution because forceful efforts to right the boat can break the mast. Be careful not to ''bounce'' the boat. Often, the assistance of a rescue boat is needed.

Diagram 42) Righting a turtled boat

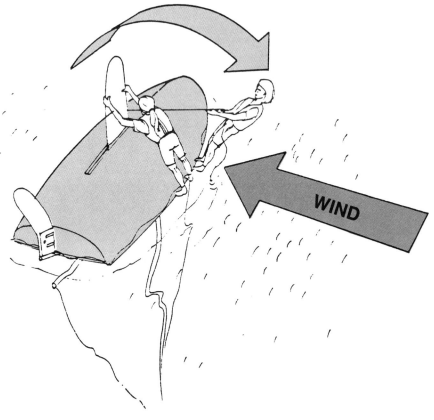

Man Overboard

Because the boat is your "survival capsule" on the water, falling overboard is a real emergency that every sailor should treat with the utmost urgency. There are a wide variety of man overboard recovery methods, but the quickest and easiest one for small boats is the **Crash Stop**. The sailor who's still onboard should immediately luff head to wind and ease off all sheets. If this is done right away, the boat will come to a stop alongside or a little to windward of the victim. The person in the water should then be helped aboard over the transom.

If it's necessary to turn and sail back to the person in the water, try to keep an eye on the victim and make a luffing approach from downwind just as in approaching the leeward side of a dock (page 68) or picking up a mooring.

Many single handed dinghies are designed to capsize promptly if the skipper falls off, but if yours is not, be sure to keep a good grip on the tiller and mainsheet.

Diagram 43) Crash stop for man overboard

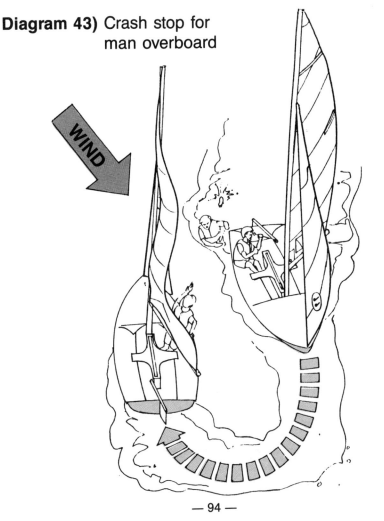

Treating Hypothermia

Hypothermia is always a potential hazard when sailing in cold or wet conditions, but it becomes much more likely following a capsize or man overboard incident. The first signs of hypothermia are the obvious ones: feeling cold and shivering. However, as the body gets colder, a person may stop feeling especially cold and will become very tired, passive and lethargic. Lips and fingernails turn blue, and speech becomes slurred. Further cooling will result in unconsciousness, and ultimately death.

If you think that you or another sailor is starting to suffer from hypothermia, put on additional dry clothes and a windbreaker if possible. Return to shore immediately. Canadian Coast Guard Search and Rescue units and some emergency medical teams have special equipment for re-warming hypothermia victims so try to get outside help if the victim is badly chilled. Severe hypothermia can easily kill.

First aid for hypothermia involves getting out of the wind, removing wet clothing, and beginning controlled re-warming. A warm bath (not too hot) is excellent, or, if no tub is available, a warm shower. Warm, nonalcoholic drinks help, but alcoholic ones stimulate blood circulation to the arms and legs, and may actually cause the core body temperature to drop more. If no warm water is available, cuddling up to the chilled victim inside a sleeping bag or blanket is a good way to assist re-warming — one that has saved lives.

Chapter 18 — The Importance of Seamanship

Key Ideas:
- Right of Way
- Judging Weather
- Wind and Waves
- Geographic Hazards
- No Wind

Seamanship is a blanket term that covers a wide variety of skills and know-how. However, the essence of seamanship is a responsible attitude toward boats and the water. Competent sailors avoid interfering with other boats, know when and where it's safe to sail, and take good care of their equipment.

Sharing the Water with Other Boats

The old rule that sail has right of way over power dates back to the days of large, hard-to-handle sailing row ships that could barely beat to windward. With a maneuverable sailing dinghy, it would be stupid (and often illegal) to try to force a commercial vessel to change course to avoid you. Get out of the way and in plenty of time.

When sailboats meet there are four basic rules that determine which boat should alter course. Don't, of course, insist on your right of way if it means a collision!

Right of Way Rule #1 — *Port tack gives way to starboard tack.*

Right of Way Rule #2 — *Windward gives way to leeward boat when both are on the same tack.*

Right of Way Rule #3 — *A faster boat must keep clear of a same tack boat that it's overtaking.*

Right of Way Rule #4 — *A boat that's tacking or gybing must keep clear of a boat that's sailing straight.*

Evaluating Weather Conditions

To develop a feel for the weather, try listening to TV or radio forecasts each day, then watching to see what actually happens. You'll soon become quite skilled at predicting the general wind and weather conditions in your local sailing area. However, squalls and thunderstorms can still be difficult to anticipate. The following list points out some of the important things to look for when it comes to weather.

Diagram 44) Basic Weather Knowledge

1) Changes in air pressure as measured by a **barometer**. A rapidly falling barometer often occurs in advance of a storm.

2) Towering, dark thunderclouds, usually plainly visible at least half an hour before strong winds, rain and lightning arrives. Use this time to head to shore as quickly as possible.

3) Line Squalls which occur quite often in some Canadian sailing areas strike with great force and little warning. All you may see is a fast approaching line of dark water as the squall races toward you. Try to take down your sails before the wind hits, but if capsized, hold tight to the boat. Squalls usually last only a few minutes.

4) Small, fluffy **cumulus** clouds and a high or rising barometer are signs of good weather. But remember, thunderstorms and squalls can still develop quickly in some areas, so keep a good lookout.

5) Foggy weather and poor visibility can cause a small boat sailor to get lost, particularly if there's no compass and chart aboard. Stay near the launching area in questionable conditions.

6) "Fish scale" **cirrus clouds** often can be seen a day or so before good weather deteriorates.

Wind And Waves

Wind blowing over water causes waves to build up, and the strength of the wind can be estimated by the size of these waves. Remember, the longer the wind lasts and the wider the expanse of water, the larger the waves tend to become; so the following guidelines are only general rules:

WIND SPEED	WAVE APPEARANCE
3 - 7 km/hr	small ripples
8 - 15 km/hr	wavelets
16 - 20 km/hr	small waves, occasional whitecaps
21 + km/hr	substantial waves, abundant whitecaps

Geographic Hazards

Specifics differ from one sailing area to another, so you should discuss possible hazards with your sailing instructor and study a local chart. Some general types of geographic hazards are:

1) Shallow water and underwater obstructions that the centreboard or daggerboard can hit. Sometimes marked by **navigational aids** such as buoys and beacons.

2) Dangerous currents caused either by downstream water flow in rivers or tidal action in sea coast areas. Strong current areas can often be spotted by unusually steep, choppy waves (wind and current opposed) or by exceptionally smooth, slick looking water (wind and current moving together).

3) Shifty, gusty winds near steep shores, behind islands, in narrow channels, or downwind of tall buildings.

When the Wind Quits

Any dinghy should be equipped with two paddles to help with close quarters maneuvering and get back to shore in a calm. Practice some paddling before you really need it, so you know how to keep the boat moving in a straight line.

Sometimes a single power boat may tow a whole fleet of becalmed sailing dinghies by trailing a long line in the water off it's stern. To hitch a ride, you need to know how to tie your painter onto this line so it holds firmly and doesn't slide back. The knot to use is called the **Rolling Hitch**.

For better control while being towed, raise the centreboard half way. Make the tow boat operator's job easier by steering a steady course toward the transom of the power boat instead of veering from side to side.

Diagram 45) Taking a tow. Painters are secured to the tow line using the rolling hitch.

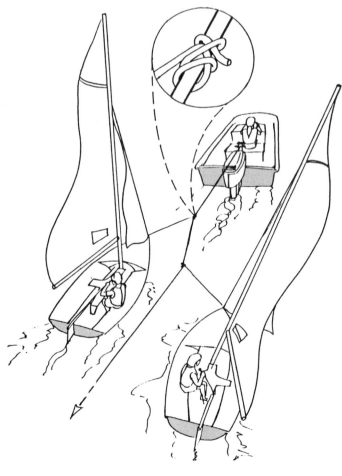

Chapter 19) Going On in Sailing

Key Ideas:
- **Organization of Sailing in Canada**
- **Advanced CYA Sail Training**
- **One Design Racing**
- **Becoming a Sailing Instructor**
- **Crewing and Cruising**

In many villages, towns and cities all across Canada, people who love sailing have gotten together to form local sailing clubs and associations. Chances are your learn-to-sail program is sponsored and operated by such a group. In some cases, associations are formed by sailors who all own, sail and race a particular kind of sailboat known as a **one design class**. A few popular one design boats are Lasers, Lightnings, Stars, Sharks and Hobie 16s, but there are hundreds of others.

Almost all local sailing clubs and associations belong to both a **Provincial Sailing Association** and the national **Canadian Yachting Association** or **CYA**. The Provincial Associations promote local sailing, and act as a liaison between individuals and clubs on the one hand and the CYA on the other.

The CYA is the national governing body serving Canadian sailing from the international down to the local levels. It sets national standards for sail training, selects the National Sailing Team, and represents sailing interests to government agencies such as the Coast Guard. The CYA also represents Canada in the International Yacht Racing Union which organizes the sport of sailboat racing worldwide.

Additional CYA Sail Training

After you have met the standards for the White Sail III, the highest level in the CYA Basic Sailing program, the next step is to enroll in a CYA Bronze Sail or Advanced Sailing program. Sailors who meet the standards for Bronze Sail IV and V will be able to sail efficiently in a wide range of wind conditions using more advanced techniques such as roll tacking, spinnaker and trapeze. In addition, they will know a great deal about boats, sails, wind, weather, and sailing equipment. In short, they will be highly qualified, self-reliant small boat sailors ready to go on to the highest levels in sailing.

The next level in the CYA sail training progression is Silver Sail VI — an introduction to one design sailboat racing. From there, you can progress to Gold Sail VII, the highest standard in the CYA sail training program and one which requires significant achievement in province wide racing. Beyond Gold Sail VII, the most promising Canadian racing sailors may seek CYA National Team membership to help them prepare for international and Olympic competition.

Another option available to those who qualify at the Bronze Sail V level or higher is to become a CYA certified sailing instructor. This is an excellent opportunity for young sailors (16 years or older) who enjoy working with people and sharing their enthusiasm for the sport. Instructor training clinics are usually organized by the Provincial Sailing Associations in conjunction with local yacht clubs.

Other Sailing Opportunities

A Bronze Sail program is well worthwhile for almost any sailor, but for those who don't aspire to go on into small boat racing or sailing instruction, there are plenty of other opportunities available. Thousands of Canadians love cruising in sailboats, and the CYA has established standards for the learn-to-cruise programs that are offered in many areas. Larger cruising type keelboats are also raced at local, regional and international levels. These big boats need large crews, so most keelboat racing skippers are always looking for keen young sailors. Check around the docks at local yacht clubs and there's a good chance you'll be invited out sailing on race days.

So for now, good luck and great sailing. Hope to see you out on the water!

WHITE SAIL - LEVEL I

On completion of White Sail I, the sailor will be able to carry out the following tasks in wind strengths of 8-15 km/hr (5-10 mph) where applicable.

THE ON THE WATER SAILING TASKS ARE TO BE PERFORMED UNDER INSTRUCTOR DIRECTION.

Terminology may be introduced as necessary leading up to the requirements in White Sail II.

ASHORE KNOWLEDGE

SECTION I — Safety

The candidate must be able to:

1. Describe when a lifejacket should be worn.

2. Put on and properly secure a Ministry of Transportation (MOT) approved lifejacket or personal flotation device (PFD) on land, demonstrating that it is:
   a) suitable for the weight and size of the wearer;
   b) in good repair;
   c) fits snugly so that it will not slip off in the water;
   d) MOT approved.

3. Describe and demonstrate the proper sailing clothing and personal equipment for the following conditions in a dinghy:
   a) hot sun;
   b) rain or wet sailing;
   c) cold weather, cold water;
   d) always - footwear, knife, lifejacket or PFD.

4. Describe the following safety actions to be followed immediately after a capsize:
   a) ensure that you are not tangled in lines;
   b) ensure the safety of crew members;
   c) attempt to keep boat from "turning turtle";
   d) keep one hand on the boat.

5. Describe how to right a capsized and turtled sailboat.

6. List from memory the MOT required items for a sailboat not over 5.5 metres long as outlined in the current Boating Safety Guide.

SECTION II — Seamanship

7. a) Without assistance, tie:
     i) a reef or square knot in five seconds;
     ii) a figure of eight know in five seconds;
     iii) a round turn and two half hitches in ten seconds;
     iv) a bowline in ten seconds.
   b) Describe the principle use of each of the above knots.

8. Describe four ways to identify from what direction the wind is blowing.

AFLOAT SKILLS

SECTION III — Preliminaries

9. Coil a line correctly.

10. Make a line fast to a cleat.

11. Under the direction of an instructor, get in and out of a boat safely at a dock or mooring. Demonstrate correct weight distribution, smooth movement, maintenance of own balance and ability to correct for weight shifts of others.

SECTION IV — Rigging

12. Single-handedly rig a training boat by rigging sails, and control lines, fitting the rudder and tiller, adjusting the centreboard and hoisting sails. (Mast is already stepped).

13. Demonstrate how to properly secure all essential gear for sailing (as a minimum the MOT list of required items) in a training boat.

SECTION V — Boat Handling (Under Instructor Direction)

14. Identify the direction of the wind.

15. Carry out simple sheet adjustments while underway to keep sail just on the point of luffing while on a reach.

16. Carry out simple rudder adjustments, keeping a boat going in a straight line on a reach for at least two minutes.

17. Demonstrate the righting of a capsized boat and clearing it of water.

SECTION VI — De-rigging and Securing

18. Secure a boat at a dock:
    a) by the bow only - use the proper size line and length of knot, secure the boat clear of hazards (other boats, rocks, power lines, etc.)
    b) by the bow and stern - according to the above standards but also using proper bow and stern lines and fenders to prevent unwanted boat movement and rubbing.

19. Secure a boat to a mooring, using the appropriate size line and knot.

20. Single-handedly unrig a training boat by lowering and removing sails, removing and stowing rudder and tiller and properly securing the boom and centreboard (where applicable).

21. Given a loose sail, with assistance spread it out free of wrinkles, fold and bag it properly.

22. Demonstrate how to properly secure all gear in a training boat following sailing (e.g. for the night).

WHITE SAIL — LEVEL II

On completion of White Sail II, the sailor will be able to carry out the following tasks in wind strengths of 8-16 km/hr (4-8 knots), where applicable.

THE ON THE WATER SAILING TASKS ARE TO BE PERFORMED UNDER INSTRUCTOR DIRECTION.

ASHORE KNOWLEDGE

SECTION I — Terminology

1. Identify the following parts of a sailboat:
   - a) hull
   - b) bow
   - c) stern
   - d) transom
   - e) mast
   - f) boom
   - g) mainsail
   - h) jib
   - i) battens
   - j) traveller/briddle
   - k) spreader
   - l) boom vang
   - m) goose neck

2. Point out and describe the functions of the following items in a sailboat:
   - a) centreboard
   - b) daggerboard
   - c) mainsheet
   - d) jib sheet
   - e) halyard
   - f) fairlead
   - g) block
   - h) shackle
   - i) cleat (describe 2 types)
   - j) forestay
   - k) shrouds
   - l) rudder
   - m) tiller
   - n) tiller extension
   - o) painter
   - p) hiking strap
   - q) bailer

3. Define the following terms:
   - a) port
   - b) starboard
   - c) tacking
   - d) gybing
   - e) windward
   - f) leeward
   - g) luffing (of sails)
   - h) heel
   - i) hiking
   - j) skipper
   - k) helmsman
   - l) crew
   - m) heading up
   - n) bearing away

4. Describe the following points of sail and select individual diagrams which show these points:
   - a) beat
   - b) head to wind
   - c) run
   - d) port tack
   - e) starboard tack
   - f) close reach
   - g) beam reach
   - h) broad reach
   - i) sailing by the lee

SECTION II — Seamanship

5. a) Without assistance, tie:
    i) rolling hitch in 20 seconds;
    ii) a sheetbend in 20 seconds.
  b) Describe the main use of each of these knots.

6. Identify and describe the wave conditions and beaufort scale resulting from the various wind strengths.

AFLOAT SKILLS

SECTION III — Boat Handling (Under Instructor Direction)

7. Act as helmsman while getting underway from, and returning to, a dock, mooring or beach.

8. Act as a crew while getting underway from and returning to a dock, mooring or beach using accepted responses to the helmsman's commands. (Optional)

9. Act as helmsman while beating, reaching, running, tacking, gybing, bearing away and heading up using proper commands.

10. Act as crew while beating, reaching, running, tacking, gybing, bearing away, and heading up, responding correctly to directions from the helmsman for sail trim, centreboard adjustment and boat trim. (Optional)

11. As helmsman, stop a boat at a predetermined point by luffing up (as in approaching a mooring).

12. As skipper and crew, right a turtled boat.

WHITE SAIL — LEVEL III

On completion of White Sail Level III the beginner sailor will be able to sail with confidence, competently and safely in wind strengths of 8-16 km/hr (4-8 knots) and be able to carry out the following skills proficiently without supervision.

THE LAND AND WATER TASKS MUST BE PERFORMED WITHOUT INSTRUCTOR DIRECTION.

ASHORE KNOWLEDGE

SECTION I — Safety

1. To be able to describe:
   a) what hypothermia is and how it is caused;
   b) three ways to minimize the dangers of hypothermia;
   c) basic rules on how to treat a mild case of hypothermia after the victim is out of the water.

2. To be able to identify and explain:

   The meaning of the colours and shapes of the lateral buoyage system

   Starboard hand buoys   Port hand buoys
   Mid channel buoys   Buoys indicating isolated dangers

3. List the local geographic and navigational hazards and describe the actions required to avoid or minimize their effects.

4. a) List three sources of local weather information.
   b) List local weather hazards, how they can be identified, the normal warning available and describe the actions to be taken to avoid or reduce their effects.

SECTION II — Terminology

5. Point to and describe the use of the following items in a sailboat:
   a) turnbuckle/shroud adjustor
   b) thwart
   c) buoyancy tank
   d) centreboard line
   e) pintle and gudgeon
   f) rudder blade
   g) rudder head
   h) mast step
   i) cotter pin
   j) clevis pin
   k) split ring

6. Point out and describe the following parts of a sail:
   a) luff   d) tack   g) batten pockets   j) cringle
   b) clew   e) head   h) bolt rope
   c) leech   f) foot   i) hanks

7. Describe the distinguising features of each of the following types of sailboats and give an example of each:
   a) cat rigged boat
   b) sloop rigged boat
   c) keeboat
   d) centreboard boat
   e) sailboard
   f) catamaran

SECTION III — Seamanship

8. Describe how to sail away from and back to:
   a) a beach with an on-shore wind;
   b) a dock for various wind directions;
   c) a mooring.

9. a) To be able to state the major function of the Canadian Yachting Association, provincial sailing associations, member yacht clubs and class associations.
   b) To be able to briefly describe the structure of the "Learn to Sail" program.

SECTION IV — Rules of the Road

10. Describe, with the use of diagrams, the Rules of the Road for prevention of collision at sea in the following situations and identify the vessel having the right of way by means of diagrams:
    a) port - starboard
    b) windward - leeward
    c) overtaking

11. Describe what common-sense action you should take when sailing in the vicinity of commercial shipping.

AFLOAT SKILLS

SECTION V — Boat Handling

12. Without instructor direction, act as skipper while sailing a boat:
    a) away from and back to a dock for various wind directions;
    b) away from and back to a mooring;
    c) on a windward/leeward course.

13. Without instructor direction, act as crew for the situations described in item 12. (This item is optional for students training for White Sail Level III in a singlehanded sailboat BUT must be completed by the student if he/she intends to enter a Bronze Sail program.)

14. Demonstrate how different skipper and crew positions affect the trim and performance of a sailboat and indicate the best positions for three given points of sail.

15. Without instructor direction, get a boat out of irons by backing the jib and main using proper rudder corrections.

16. Singlehandedly paddle a sailboat a distance of 30 metres (100 feet) without the use of a rudder. The boat must remain within 3 metres (10 feet) of either side of the direct track. (This should be carried out in light winds only. Rudder should be removed or lashed amidships.)

17. Demonstrate the following towing procedures:
    a) proper means to receive, secure and cast off a towline;
    b) correct towing points on a sailboat;
    c) proper securing inboard of a towline to a boat astern;
    d) correct boat trim, steering procedures and crew alertness while on the tow and while releasing from the tow.

18. Demonstrate the actions to be taken if the crew falls overboard, with the boat under sail, from the time the person falls overboard without warning until the crew is safely recovered. Speed, while important, is secondary to safety in performing this rescue.

19. Steer a boat purposely by the lee for 90 metres (100 yards) without gybing.

20. Without instructor direction or assistance, right a turtled boat and continue sailing.

21. Without instructor direction, sail a triangular/windward/leeward race with a timed start.

Glossary

A

Abeam — Located at right angles to the boat's mid-line.

Aft — Toward the stern.

Amidships — Near the middle of the hull.

Anchor — Hook-like device used to secure a boat to the bottom.

Anemometer — Instrument to measure wind speed.

Astern — See Aft.

Athwartships — See Abeam.

B

Bailer — Device used to empty water from the cockpit or hull of a boat.

Ballast — Weight carried by a boat to give it stability. Large boats usually have a heavy keel for ballast, while dinghies are ballasted by the weight of their crews.

Barometer — Instrument for measuring changes in air pressure.

Batten — Stiff wood or plastic strip used to support the leech of a sail.

Beam — The width of a boat.

Beam Reach — Sailing a course about 90 degrees to the wind direction

Bear Away — See Head Down.

Bear Off — See Head Down.

Beating — Beating to Windward. see Close Hauled sailing.

Block — Sailor's term for a pulley. Has one or more wheels called sheaves.

Block and Tackle — See Tackle.

Bolt Rope — Rope sewn along the luff and foot of a mainsail which slips into a groove in the spars.

Boom — Horizontal spar used to hold out the foot of a sail, especially a mainsail.

Boom Vang — Tackle leading downward from the boom which minimizes mainsail twist by preventing the boom from lifting.

Bow — The front end of a boat.

Broad Reach — Sailing with the wind coming over one corner of the stern.

By-the-Lee — Running with the wind on the same side as the boom. Generally undesireable because of the increased risk of an accidental gybe.

C

Capsizing — Tipping a boat on its side or upside down (see Turtling).

Cast Off — To release the line or lines securing the boat to a dock or mooring.

Cat — Short for Catamaran.

Catamaran — A boat with two narrow hulls connected by struts or a solid deck.

Catboat — A boat with only a mainsail.

Centreboard — **1.** A blade of wood or metal which extends through a slot in the bottom of the boat to prevent side slipping while sailing. See Daggerboard **2.** Specifically a pivoting blade serving the above purpose which swings back and up for storage, beaching etc.

Centreboard Trunk — A narrow waterproof box, open at the bottom, which contains the centreboard.

Chart — Nautical map showing geographic features, navigational aids, and hazards.

C-gybe — Poorly controlled gybe in which the boat swings through a C-shaped course. Syn. Crash Gybe, Flying Gybe, Slam Gybe.

Cleat — Mechanical device which grips or holds lines.

Clevis Pin — Removeable metal pin used to link together components of a boat's standing rigging.

Clew — Lower, aft corner of a sail.

Close Hauled — Sailing with the sheets pulled in all the way in order to approach an upwind destination as quickly as possible.

Close Reach — Sailing with the wind forward of the beam, but with the sails eased out somewhat from the close hauled position.

Cockpit — The open area in a sailboat where the skipper and crew either sit or put their feet.

Come About — Act of turning the boat into the wind until the sails re-fill from the other side. See Tacking.

Compass — Instrument used to tell directions on the water, especially when no landmarks are visible.

Control Line — Any rope used to adjust or trim a sail.

Cotter Pin — Small secondary pin used to prevent a clevis pin from accidently slipping out while sailing.

Course — The direction a boat is travelling.

Crash Gybe — See C-Gybe.

Crew — Person or people who help the skipper sail a boat.

Cringle — Sturdy ring at the corner of a sail to which a halyard or sheet is attached.

Current — Water movement caused by tides, downstream flow in rivers, etc.

D

Daggerboard — A wood or metal blade that extends and retracts vertically through a slot in the boat's bottom. Similar in function to a centreboard.

Deck — The watertight upper surface of hull.

De-Rigging — Putting away the sails and other sailing equipment after coming in off the water.

Dinghy — Small sailboat operated by one to three persons and stabilized by crew weight.

Downwind — Directly away from the source of the wind.

Dry Dunk — see Walkover Recovery

E

Ease — To let out a sheet or other control line.

F

Fairlead — Ring or U-shaped fitting which guides a control line and helps prevent tangles.

Fall Off — See Head Down

Feathering — See Pinching

Flying Gybe — See C-Gybe

Foot — The lower edge of a sail.

Fore — Associated with the bow.

Forestay — Support wire which keeps the mast from falling backward and on sloops, supports the luff of the jib.

G

Getting Underway — Starting up a boat from a standstill. See Way.

Gooseneck — Hinged fitting which links the boom to the mast.

Gunwale — Outer edge of the deck. Syn. Rail.

Gudgeons — Parts of take-apart rudder hinges which are mounted on the transom. See Pintles.

Gust — An abrupt increase in wind speed.

Gybe — Changing tacks while sailing downwind.

"Gybe Ho" — Command given by skipper to perform a gybe. Syn. "Gybing".

H

Halliard — Alternative spelling for Halyard.

Halyard — Control line used to hoist a sail and hold it up.

"Hard-a-Lee" — Alternative command for "Helm's-a-Lee", but misleading because it incorrectly suggests that the tiller should be shoved over abruptly when coming about.

Harden Up — See Head Up.

Head — Upper corner of a sail.

Head Board — Plastic or metal stiffener at the head of a sail.

Head Down — Turning a sailboat away from the source of the wind. Syn. Bear Off, Bear Away, Head Off, Fall Off.

Heading — The direction a boat is pointed. Syn. Course.

Head-to-Wind — Aiming the bow of the boat directly toward the source of the wind. See No-Go Zone.

Heat Exhaustion — Illness associated with elevated body temperature and caused by sun, heat, high humidity and dehydration.

Heel — Sideways leaning or tipping of a boat, usually caused by the force of the wind on the sails.

Helm — The tiller or steering wheel of a sailboat.

Helm's-a-Lee — Command given by the skipper when the tiller is moved to leeward to come about. Syn. Hard-a-Lee.

Helmsman — Person who steers a boat. See Skipper.

High Side — See Windward side.

Hiking — Leaning backward over the windward rail to counteract heel.

Hiking Stick — See Tiller Extension.

Hiking Straps — Foot straps which enable skipper and crew to lean back further without falling overboard.

Hole (in the wind) — See Lull.

Hull — The main shell or body of a boat.

I

In Irons — Having the boat trapped bow to wind and temporarily unable to turn onto either tack.

In Stays — See In Irons.

Inshore — Close to shore or in sheltered waters.

J

Jib — Small sail set ahead of the mast.

Jibe — Alternative spelling for Gybe.

K

Keel — Non-retractable underwater fin of a large sailboat which not only prevents side slipping, but houses ballast to provide stability.

Knot — 1. Method of attaching a line to an object or another line.
   2. Speed of one nautical mile per hour.

L

Leech — Rear edge of a sail extending from head to clew.

Leeward — Away from the source of the wind.

Leeward Side — Side of a boat that the wind passes last.

Leeway — Side slipping or crabbing motion of a sailboat, most evident on a close hauled course.

Life Jacket — Personal floation device with a buoyant collar designed to keep a victim's head above the waves. See PFD.

Life Vest — General term for a Life Jacket or PFD.

Line — A rope that has a specific function aboard a boat such as a sheet or halyard.

Line Squall — See Squall.

Low Side — See Leeward Side.

Luff — 1. The forward edge of a sail extending from head to tack 2. To cause a sail to flutter by heading up or easing the sheet.

Luff Rope — See Bolt Rope.

Luff Up — See Head Up.

Luffing — To steer or trim the sail so it flutters, either near its leading edge or over the whole sail. Syn. Feathering, Pinching.

Lull — Abrupt decrease in wind speed. Syn. Hole.

M

Main — See Mainsail.

Mainsail — Large sail set behind the mast. The only sail on a catboat.

Mast — Vertical spar which supports the sails.

Masthead — Top of the mast.

Masthead Fly — See Masthead Wind Indicator

Masthead Wind Indicator — Small weather vane mounted atop the mast.

MOB — Stands for Man Overboard - a person who has fallen overboard and in need of rescue.

Mooring — Permanant anchor connected to a buoy by rope or chain where a boat can be tied up.

Multihull — A Catamaran or Trimaran.

N

No-Go Zone — The area within wind angles extending approximately 45° to each side of upwind in which a boat cannot sail even when close hauled.

O

Off the Wind — Sailing on a reach or run.

Offshore — Far from shore or on the open ocean.

Offshore Wind — Wind blowing from the land toward the water.

Offwind — Sailing on a reach or run. Syn. Off the Wind.

On the Wind — See Close Hauled.

One Design — Racing sailboat constructed to be identical to others in its class.

Onshore Wind — Wind blowing toward the land.

Outhaul — Control that attaches the clew of a mainsail to the boom and tensions the foot of the mainsail.

P

Painter — Line at the bow of a boat used to secure the boat to a dock or mooring.

PFD — Stands for Personal Floation Device - generally a comfortable lightweight type with a low collar designed to be worn at all times and not just in emergencies. See Life Jacket.

Pinching — **1.** Steering with the sails are on the verge of luffing. When done intentionally in strong winds to avoid excessive heel it's also known as Feathering. **2.** Sailing close hauled on a course that's higher than the optimal one.

Pintles — Hinge fittings attached to the rudder that engage with mating fitting (Gudgeons) on the boat's transom.

Planing — Exciting, high speed sailing when the boat starts to skim along on the top of the water.

Playing the Sail — Keeping the sail at the best angle to the wind by alternately easing and pulling in the sheet. Syn. Trimming the Sail.

Points of Sail — Different headings of a sailboat with respect to the wind. See Close Hauled, Close Reach, Beam Reach, Broad Reach and Run.

Port — The left side of a boat as viewed facing forward.

Port Tack — Sailing with the boom on the starboard side.

"Prepare to Tack" — See "Ready About".

Puff — See Gust

R

Rail — See Gunwale.

Reaching — Sailing with the wind coming over the side of the boat, but not as far foreward as when close hauled.

"Ready About" — Command alerting the crew that the skipper intends to come about.

"Ready to Tack" — See "Ready About".

Rig — **1.** To prepare a boat for sailing **2.** The spars, sails, shrouds, stays and control lines of a sailboat.

Right of Way — In a situation where two boats converge, the one which is not obligated to alter course is said to have Right of Way.

Rudder — Hinged blade mounted at the stern of a boat which is used for steering.

Run — Sailing directly away from the wind. Syn. Downwind Sailing, Running Before the Wind.

Running Rigging — see Control Lines.

S

Sail — Cloth airfoil that works like a vertical wing to deflect the wind and produce the force which propels a sailboat.

Sailboard — Small sports boat with a hinged rig which the operator holds by hand while standing upright

Sail Trim — Adjusting the sails to take best advantage of the wind.

Scoop Recovery — Method of righting a capsized boat while, at the same time, "scooping" one crew member into the cockpit.

Self-Bailers — See Bailers.

Self-Bailing — Draining of water out of the cockpit through openings in the hull or transom.

Self-Reliance — The ability to handle varying sailing conditions with confidence and skill.

Self-Rescue — Righting a capsized boat and getting it sailing again without outside assistance.

Set — **1.** Raising and trimming a sail **2.** the direction a current is flowing.

S-Gybe — Preferred method of gybing in which the boat follows an S-shaped path because the skipper momentarily reverses the helm as the boom swings across.

Shackle — U-shaped metal link closed with a removeable pin. Often used to join lines, sails and fittings.

Sheet — **1.** Line used to control the angle of a sail to the hull **2.** Act of adjusting a sail using its sheet.

Sheet In — To pull in a sheet. Syn. Bring In, Trim.

Sheet Out — To let out a sheet. Syn. Ease Let Off

Sheeting — Playing the Sail.

Shrouds — Wire ropes which support the mast from side to side. See Standing rigging.

Singlehander — Sailboat operated by just one person.

Skipper — The person who steers and is in charge of a sailboat.

Slam Gybe — See C-Gybe.

Sloop — Single masted sailboat with two principle sails, a main and a jib.

Spar — A Mast or Boom.

Spinnaker — Lightweight parachute-like sail used on reaching and downwind courses

Squall — Very strong wind lasting just a short time

Standing Rigging — Wires and related fittings used to support the mast, but not ordinarily adjusted while sailing.

Starboard — The right hand side of a boat when looking forward.

Stay — A wire rope supporting the mast in the fore-and-aft plane. See Forestay.

Stern — The back of a boat.

Stowing — Securing or putting away sailing equipment.

T

Tack — **1.** The lower front corner of a sail **2.** The side of the boat opposite the boom (i.e. port tack, starboard tack) **3.** Syn. for Come About

Tacking — see Coming About

Tackle — An arrangement of blocks and line that multiplies force. Commonly seen in dinghy mainsheets and boom vangs.

Telltales — **1.** Short pieces of yarn, ribbon or tape attached to the shrouds to indicate wind direction **2.** Pieces of yarn or tape attached near the luff of the sail to show air flow (see Ticklers)

Thwart — Horizontal brace that supports the centreboard trunk and also serves as a seat for the crew.

Tidal Current — Water flow produced by the rise or fall of the tide.

Tide — The rise and fall in sea level caused by the gravitational pull of the moon and sun.

Tiller — Handle attached to the top of the rudder which is used to steer the boat.

Tiller Extension — Stick attached to the end of the tiller which allows the skipper to sit further out to help stabilze the boat. Syn. Hiking Stick.

Transom — The flat portion of the hull that spans the back of a boat.

Traveller — A track or rope bridle used to control the side-to-side position where the mainsheet or other control attaches to the hull.

Trim — To adjust a sail using its sheet or other controls. See Playing the Sail.

Trimaran — Boat with three side-by-side hulls. In most cases, the centre hull is the largest while the outer hulls provide stability.

Turnbuckle — Screw action adjuster used to change the length and tension of a shroud or stay.

Turtling — Capsizing until the mast points straight down.

U

Upwind — Toward the source of the wind or against the wind.

V

Vang — see Boom Vang

W

Walkover Recovery — Capside recovery where the skipper climbs over the windward rail and onto the centreboard, and, as the boat rights, back into the cockpit — all without getting wet. Syn. Dry Dunk.

Way — The movement of a boat. See Getting Underway.

Weather Side — Syn. Windward Side.

Wind Sense — Judging the speed and direction of the wind.

Windward — Toward the source of the wind Syn. To Weather.

Windward Side — The side of a boat that the wind passes first.

Wing on Wing — Sailing downwind with the jib and mainsail set on opposite sides to catch more wind.